RICHARD THOMAS PARKER

The last man to be publicly hanged in Nottingham

by

Emmaline Severn

© Emmaline Severn 2021

All rights reserved.
No part of this publication may be reproduced without prior permission of the author

Cover image: Shutterstock/holwichaikawee

ISBN 978-1-7385568-1-6

Lost Voices Publishing
www.the-field-detectives.com

CONTENTS

Preface

Dedication

INTRODUCTION

THE VILLAGES WHERE THEY LIVED

THE PARKERS EARLY YEARS

ELIZABETH'S EARLY LIFE

RICHARD THOMAS PARKER

OH, DEAR! HE'S GOT THE GUN

THE PETTY SESSIONS

TRANSCRIPTION OF POST-MORTEM REPORT

THE INQUEST

THE TRIAL

EFFORTS TO GAIN A REPRIEVE

THE END IS NIGH

THE EXECUTION

RICHARD THOMAS PARKER POSTSCRIPT

Acknowledgements

References

About the Author

Preface

This is a historical account of the events leading up to the hanging of Richard Thomas Parker on Wednesday the 10th of August 1864. His crime: the wilful murder of his mother, Elizabeth Parker, at Fiskerton, Nottinghamshire. Parker was twenty-nine years old and the last man to be publicly hanged in Nottingham.

Richard Thomas Parker was my first cousin, four times removed, and the knowledge of his heinous crime has been passed down my family line through the generations. After months of research, I felt compelled to piece together my findings in this book to provide the reader with a comprehensive version of events.

Emmaline Severn
2021

Dedication

To my dear mother, who told me the story.

My husband, for his unique ability to draw attention to himself over garden walls.

And for our ancestors - where would we be without them?

INTRODUCTION

Richard Thomas Parker was the only son of Samuel and Elizabeth Parker, born in 1834. They married late in life and lived on a small farm in Fiskerton, Nottinghamshire, close to the banks of the River Trent. All accounts of their son relate him to have been utterly indulged from childhood, so much so that he grew up a spoilt, wild young man who drank heavily and showed violent tendencies when drunk. When sober, he was quite the opposite, described as being good-looking and intelligent, with a promising future. However, fuelled by life's cycle of events, his behaviour became increasingly dissipated, eventually leading to the fateful and tragic evening of Tuesday the 29th of March 1864.

Parker often quarrelled with his father, and they came to blows on more than one occasion, with his mother, Elizabeth, usually being the mediator. This particular evening young Parker had returned home in a state of intoxication. Yet another argument blew up, the result of which led to the son firing both barrels of a shotgun at his parents. His father Samuel recovered from his injuries, but his mother lingered on for several weeks before she died.

Richard Thomas Parker was tried and found guilty of wilful murder at Nottinghamshire County Court. He was hanged on Wednesday the 10th of August 1864 upon gallows outside the County Gaol, now home to the National Justice Museum.

What follows is a narrative of the days leading to the tragic event and those leading to the execution. Accounts written in the Nottingham Journal and the Nottinghamshire Guardian are the primary sources of information pertaining to events of the murder, the trial and the hanging, alongside other documents deposited at the Nottinghamshire Archives and Nottingham University Manuscripts and Special Collections. Any family history included is from the author's own research.

Quotations in italics as part of the text are from either/or:
Nottingham Journal - Periodicals 29th July 1864 and 12th August 1864
Source: Manuscripts and Special Collections, University of Nottingham
Nottingham Guardian Supplement - Source: www.britishnewspaperarchive.co.uk

THE VILLAGES WHERE THEY LIVED

Our villages in question are Fiskerton, Bleasby and Thurgarton, which all lie approximately eleven to fourteen miles northeast of Nottingham and run close by the river Trent. Each village has its own history and was home to the families whose own histories will unfold.

FISKERTON is a small village, and the name was derived from the Saxon word *'fiskr'* meaning fish, the addition of the suffix *'tun'* gives us *'the farm of the fisherman,'* and to this day, it is still a popular place for fisherman. Many centuries ago, the River Trent was fordable at Fiskerton, and indeed the armies of Henry VII and the Earl of Lincoln crossed here on the 16th of June 1487 and met at Stoke Field to fight the last battle of the War of the Roses. The site is known as Red Gutter due to the bloody carnage that took place.

Over time, the village's closeness to the river encouraged other industries to develop. Alongside farming and fishing, various warehouses, coal yards and wharves were set up by the riverside, with malting also becoming a local industry. A ferry crossing has existed at Fiskerton, situated opposite the Bromley Arms, since the days of the Domesday Book and was still in use until the 1950s.

BLEASBY is also a typical village of rural England and has the site of another ancient crossing point close by, known as Hazelford Ferry. One of the earliest mentions of Bleasby dates to AD 627 during the reign of the pagan King Edwin of Northumbria. He wanted to marry Ethelburg, the daughter of Ethelbert, the king of Kent, however, Ethelbert would only allow the marriage if Edwin converted to Christianity. This he eventually agreed to do and following their marriage, which unified the whole of England for the first time, Edwin's court reputedly turned up in Bleasby, the Trent considered as being halfway between Kent and Northumbria. Here they were all baptised in the shallow waters by Paulinus, a Roman priest, who later became the first Archbishop of York.

A terrible plague visited Bleasby in 1604, which carried off eighty-seven out of a population of probably less than 300. The parish register contains entries for sometimes two or three burials in a day, and although there is no cause of death mentioned, in nearby Fiskerton, a death from 'pestis suspecta' (plague suspected) was recorded. On the following day, when in the same household another death occurred, entered in the list of burials were the words 'pestis confessa' (plague confirmed). The outbreak was possibly very local, as there is no mention of it in any other neighbouring parishes. A few months after the outbreak, the bereaved began to re-marry, and the population started to increase.

THURGARTON has an ancient history that includes the founding of a priory in the 12th century, home to the Austin or Black Canons. Today only the priory's cellars remain beneath a Georgian mansion built in the mid-18th century. The 1861 census lists the population as being mostly agricultural labourers, cottagers and farmers, with butchers and a blacksmith, alongside the other usual occupations required for day-to-day living in a rural village at that time.

Although each village is within walking distance of each other, when the Nottingham to Lincoln railway opened in August 1846, serving each of our villages of interest, travel further afield opened up new opportunities to many folk.

Today they are mainly commuter villages and places to visit for a walk by the river and enjoy a pleasant Sunday lunch at the local pub.

1884 ORDNANCE SURVEY MAP OF THE VILLAGES
Reproduced with the permission of the National Library of Scotland

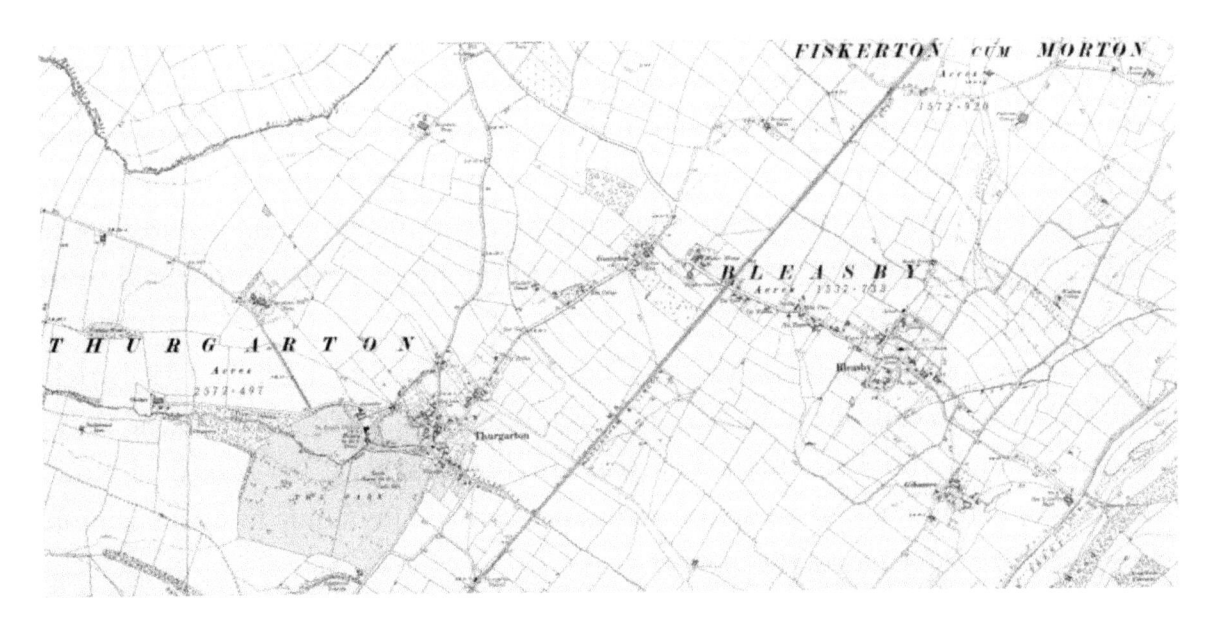

THE PARKERS EARLY YEARS

For many generations, the Parker family lived in Bleasby with William Parker and Anne Dixon, being their forebears. They wed at the village church of St Mary's in 1716, and their marriage bond informs us that William was a farmer at the time of their marriage. The family continued to add colour to the village and surrounding area for another hundred years or more.

Fast forward a couple of generations to the union of John Parker and Ann Freeman on the 21st of February 1792 at St Mary's, Bleasby. They produced twelve children, including Samuel Parker, born in 1802, father of the Fiskerton Murder Perpetrator.

Samuel's eldest brother, John, born 1792, continued the farming tradition, and the 1851 census informs us that he farmed about twenty-seven acres adjacent to Bleasby church. The draft Enclosure Map of c1780 shows John's house and land alongside other fields in Bleasby that he rented from the Retford Corporation. Although farming was a hard life during the 19th century, he lived to the age of seventy-nine, eventually dying in 1871. He left effects of under £1500 (*equivalent in 2020 = £140,700*), distributed amongst his own immediate family. A further development connected to John's estate will be revealed later in the narrative.

Another of the brothers, Thomas, born 1804, is described in the 1851 census as a 'retired butcher' aged forty-seven, living in Sneinton. In the 1861 census, Thomas is recorded as a Gentleman, a word loosely used in this era to describe one as 'not working' and or 'living off own means.' He appeared to have accumulated sufficient funds to retire relatively young, and the sum of his estate after his death in 1881 amounted to £396.10 (*equivalent in 2020 = £40,290*) after deductions for mortgage debts on leaseholds were bequeathed to his brother, Samuel.

One of the younger brothers, Matthew, born 1809, embarked upon the wheelwright trade and spent his early life in Bleasby, however, he married in Nottingham at St Mary's Church in 1833 and lived for a few years in Packer's Place on Mansfield Road, Nottingham. From the 1841 census onwards, Matthew and his family lived in Sneinton, close to his brother Thomas, the butcher.

Of Samuel's other numerous siblings, William became a shoemaker, and Richard a farm labourer. Sadly, three of the sisters died in their twenties and thirties, but the remaining sisters married and lived long and hopefully happy lives. Charlotte was born in 1814 and married a butcher. They continued the butchery business in Bleasby, also taking on a farm later. After Charlotte became widowed in 1875, she took over running the farm, which covered 118 acres, until her death in 1900, aged eighty-six.

As for Samuel, father of the perpetrator, it would seem he spent his early life as a farm labourer, and the Nottingham Journal reported he *'occupied a farm in Farndon,'* Nottinghamshire prior to his meeting and marrying Elizabeth, mother of the young man who ended her life.

PARKER FAMILY TREE

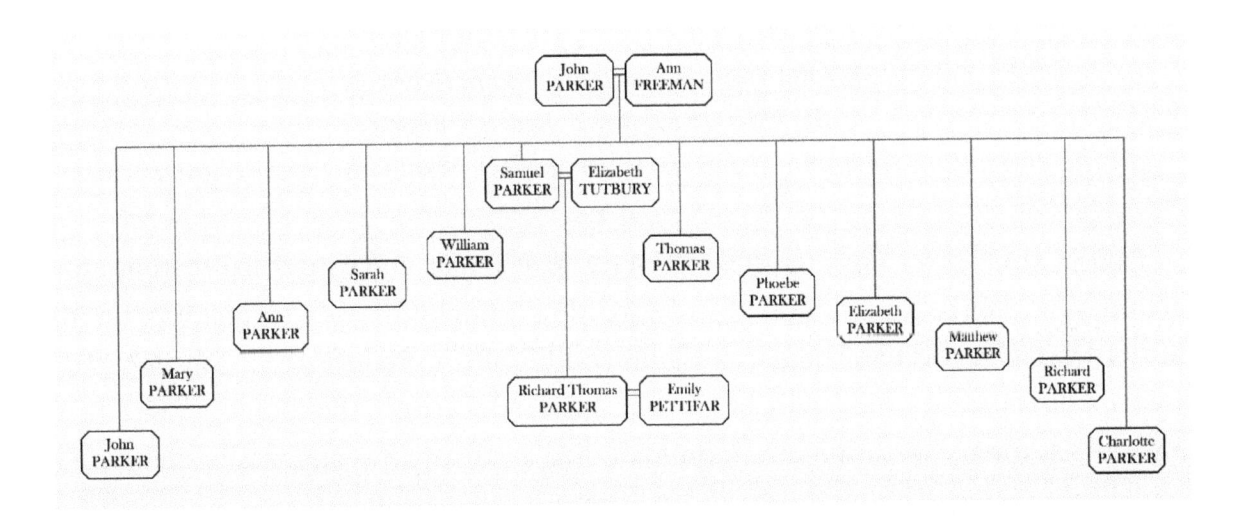

ELIZABETH'S EARLY LIFE

Elizabeth was baptised on the 9th of November 1789 at St Mary's and All Saints, Bingham, the daughter of William and Anne Tutbury. She proved to be an enterprising young lady who married an older man named John Hart, a farmer and innkeeper from Thurgarton. John had already been married and widowed twice, including a marriage to Elizabeth's aunt. Whilst it might not be illegal for a man to marry the niece of his dead wife, it may have been frowned upon in the late 18th century. Furthermore, not only was Elizabeth his niece and thirty-one years his junior, but at the time of their marriage, she was also most probably pregnant, hence perhaps their elopement to Sculcoates, Yorkshire, a marriage licence, and a hasty wedding.

[1]John Hart wid of the parish of Thurgarton and Elizth Tutbury Spin of this parish were married in this church by licence from Revd J Bromby this 31st day of March in the year 1811 - By me Rd Patrick vicar
This marriage was solemnized between us
John Hart and E X (her mark) Tutbury
In the presence of {Hannah X (her mark) Woodlass, Wm X (his mark) Lowther of Lincoln

And so, the happy couple returned to Thurgarton as man and wife. Their firstborn son arrived very close to nine months after the wedding, with his baptism taking place on the 8th of December 1811 at Thurgarton. John and Elizabeth produced four sons together: John, William, Henry and James, but the age difference between the couple left Elizabeth a widow at the age of thirty-four. John Hart died aged sixty-five and was buried on the 6th of July 1823, and on his death, he left Elizabeth *'quite comfortable.'*

His last will and testament was written four days before his burial, probably drawn up whilst he lay upon his death bed. Elizabeth and her young sons were left in a secure position, with the farm to live and work on, alongside property and rents providing a steady income. Stipulations were made as to what went where and how much to whom, but principally, Elizabeth was to keep the farm until her eldest son became twenty-one, after which he would inherit. His mother was then to receive an annuity of £20, or £15 (*equivalents in 2020 = £1826 and £1369*) if she re-married. The three younger sons were to receive £500 (*equivalent in 2020 = £45,640*) each when they reached twenty-one.

From the Nottinghamshire Guardian report, we are told that the eldest son John was reputedly an invalid and lived with his brother William, the second son. The census return confirms that William had taken over running the farm with John recorded as 'brother' to the head of the household. Subsequently, this meant that William dealt with any future transactions connected to the farm and properties.

It is not known when Samuel Parker entered the life of the widowed Mrs Hart, but he was most likely in his late twenties when he began working for her on the farm, being described as a *'labourer of the better class.'* Despite Elizabeth being thirteen years older than Samuel, she was evidently a woman possessed of a *'large share of personal attractions, well-formed, graceful and of a genial, affectionate nature.'*

Elizabeth is listed in the 1832 White's Directory as a farmer in Thurgarton, and having a young family to care for, together with the running of the farm, she found herself unable to manage the business on her own. Therefore, she entrusted Samuel as a sort of steward on the farm. He was described as *'distinguished by much energy and character, scrupulous honesty and at this period of his life was a strong, athletic and handsome man.'*

Friendship between the couple blossomed into love, and thus, Samuel and Elizabeth married by licence on the 1st of March 1834 at St Mary's, Nottingham. Samuel was thirty-two years old; Elizabeth was now forty-five and pregnant.

Their beloved son, Richard Thomas Parker, was baptised on the 26th of October 1834 at St Peter's, Thurgarton.

The Nottinghamshire Guardian informs us that Elizabeth's farm and business were left to one of her sons from her first marriage, whom we now know to be William. Thus, it can be assumed that sometime after this, Samuel and Elizabeth Parker moved to Fiskerton.

Elizabeth must have remained 'comfortable' after her marriage to Samuel, as the newspapers reported he owned his own house and some of the adjoining tenements. He was also the owner of several acres of freehold land. All in all, the Parkers were said to be a respectable family in the area.

Samuel and Elizabeth lived in *'a small modern built farm-house facing into a garden, with the back to the street,'* overlooking the River Trent, within the vicinity of the Spread

Eagle public house and the Bromley Arms. Elizabeth's first husband, John Hart, had owned land adjacent to the property in and around 1808, which had been transferred into the Parker name by 1837. Samuel then purchased the house for £210 (*equivalent in 2020 = £19,240*) in 1841 from William Hart, Mrs Parker's son from her first marriage. Indeed, most of the buildings within the Spread Eagle Yard belonged to the Hart and Parker families at this point in time.

The full history of the various owners of this land and property can be found in an Abstract of Title document held at the Nottinghamshire Archives ref: DD/899/3

1884 ORDNANCE SURVEY MAP OF FISKERTON SHOWING THE LOCATION OF THE SPREAD EAGLE YARD AND THE PARKER'S HOUSE
Reproduced with the permission of the National Library of Scotland

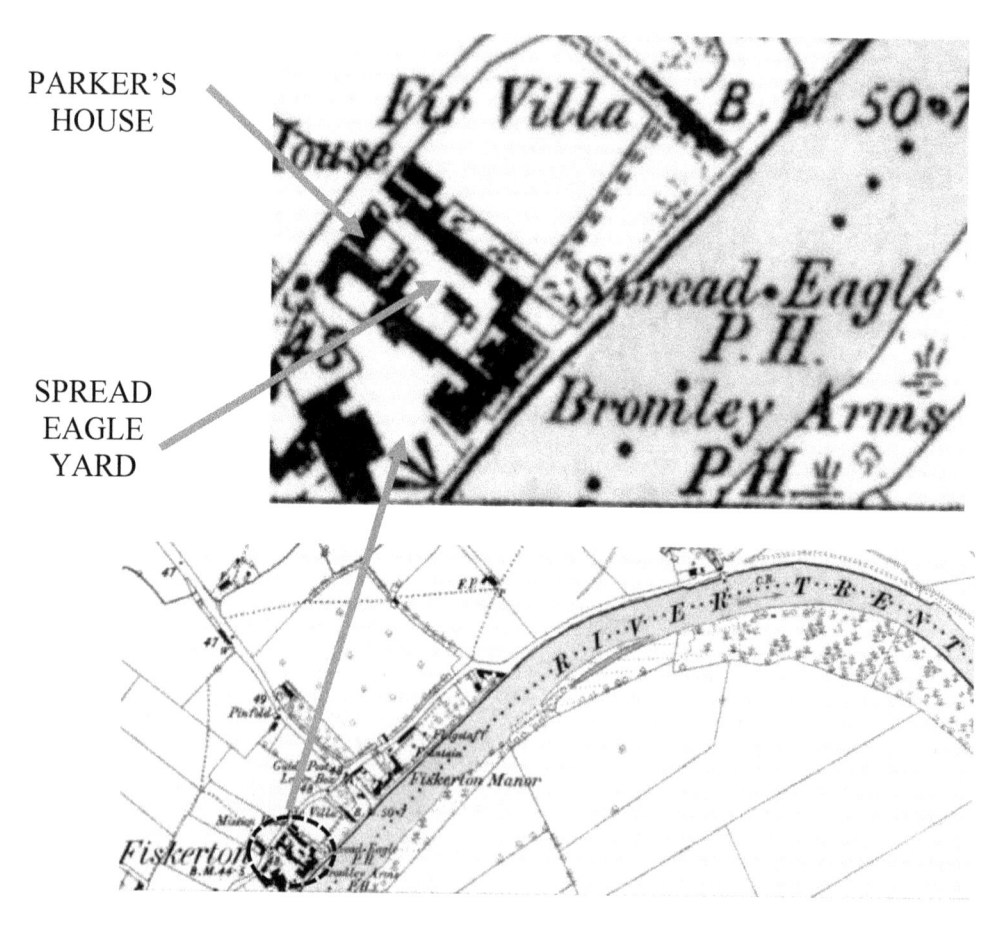

RICHARD THOMAS PARKER

Known as Tom, it is said he was thoroughly spoilt and overindulged as a child, described as having always been headstrong and violent. He grew up in Fiskerton, and rumours of his violence were reported later with tales such as, 'when playing in a cricket match with a neighbouring village he was offended by one of the opposite side and stabbed him in the arm.' Whether these stories were true or not is debatable.

At the age of eighteen, Tom was apprenticed to a butcher named Mr Bee on Sneinton Street, Nottingham. One could worry about a potentially violent man entering the butchery trade, brandishing knives and cleavers.

According to the newspapers, having completed his apprenticeship, he returned to Fiskerton and was given a butcher's shop opposite his parent's house, a further indulgence one could suspect. The Nottingham Journal report suggested that he initially made a success of his business, however, the more colourful Nottingham Guardian tells that he *'indulged in behaviour of the wildest dissipation, neglecting his business completely.'* His morals were reported to have been somewhat loose and that he had even fathered an illegitimate child in Nottingham.

In an effort to steady him down, Parker's parents found him a suitable young woman, and thus Emily Pettifar, said to have been of *'superior manners'*, was introduced to Parker. They married on the 24th of September 1860 at St Mary's, Newark, Nottinghamshire. Their first child Julia was baptised on the 14th of July 1861. The dates are close, but it looks as though Emily was probably pregnant at the time of the marriage.

A year later, they had a son, Samuel, baptised on the 9th of November 1862. Both baptisms took place at St Mary's, Newark.

Parker treated Emily brutally from the start, and the Nottingham Guardian describes how *'Her life as long as she remained with her husband was the reverse of a happy one. On the first night of their wedded life, he assaulted her and a day or two later threw over her a large quantity of water.'* The Nottingham Journal adds that *'On one occasion he came home in the evening in a state of intoxication and turned his wife into the street in her nightclothes.'*

They separated repeatedly, but Emily was always persuaded back by Tom's parents with promises that he would change. However, before long, his drinking became so bad and the beatings too cruel that, not surprisingly, she fled, taking their two children to live with her father in Newark.

Parker appeared before the magistrates at the Southwell Quarter Sessions on the 11th of September 1863, charged with assaulting Emily on the 27th of August at Fiskerton.

'Mr Heathcote appeared for the defendant. After a long hearing, the magistrates advised them to settle the case, and the defendant agreed to allow his wife 6s a week and to pay the whole of the costs.' (equivalent of 6s in 2020 = £28.92)

So, by September 1863, with his business and marriage of only three years in tatters, Parker returned to his parents' house and was supposed to help his now elderly father with the farm. Fights between father and son were frequent, usually started by arguments over young Parker's behaviour. With Parker senior being also of an *'excitable nature, who enjoyed a drink or two and who still possessed great strength despite his age,'* they would often come to blows.

The Nottingham Guardian reported that *'Parker's unhappy father is admittedly a very excitable man and although he has never exhibited positive symptoms of aberration of intellect, his brothers, the uncles of the condemned were notoriously insane, and insanity is hereditary in the family.'*

The word 'insanity' seems to have been bandied about quite loosely in times gone by, and why this conclusion was reached is unknown and perhaps not too convincing a declaration. All of the uncles appear to have worked productively throughout their lives, making it into their seventies and eighties, so if insane meant 'colourful characters', then it might have been fun to meet them. However, one would have to have been there at the time to make an informed judgment.

Thus, the scene is set leading up to the fateful evening of Tuesday the 29th of March 1864.

OH, DEAR! HE'S GOT THE GUN

The day before, Monday the 28th of March, Tom Parker had asked his seventy-four-year-old mother if he could take leave to go to Sheffield. The Bradfield Reservoir had burst causing a terrible flood, killing 240 people and causing catastrophic destruction. The disaster became known as the Great Inundation and special trains were arranged to take 'sightseers' from all around the country to visit the devastation. Parker, among the rest, was seized with a desire to see the scene of the tragedy.

Evidently, his conduct during the visit showed that he was *'not properly impressed by the devastation of which he saw the evidences lying around. He appears to have partaken freely of drink and was so violent that a police officer was set to keep watch on his proceedings, and he narrowly escaped being arrested and locked up.'*

His father, Samuel, had been against the idea of his son attending as he needed him to help on the farm. Still, his mother agreed he could go, but rather than returning home that evening as agreed, Tom travelled to Newark, where he stayed all night so that he could attend the Stock (Cattle) Market in the morning. At the close of the market, he was seen in a *'state of intoxication.'*

He then went to the cricket match being played on the field, and it would appear that: *'During his stay in Newark he drank a great deal and as might be expected from one of his disposition and tendencies, he brought himself to that condition in which the least provocation was calculated to drive him to a frenzy.'*

The next morning, a policeman to whom Parker was known, crossed paths with him in the Market Place, and he was still not sober. On seeing that Parker was missing his collar, the policeman *'recommended him to go into an outfitter's shop and purchase one.'* Parker did comply, but several people saw him that morning and *'some of his acts and expressions denoted the desperate and almost maniacal state of mind in which he was.'*

He had also attempted to see his children in Newark but had been refused. This led to an angry outburst where Parker *'got possession of the child from the nurse and appeared determined not to give it up, but was at length persuaded to do so, principally by the unwillingness of the infant to remain with him.'*

He then threatened to shoot his father-in-law, George Pettifar, after which arguments on the train journey home to Fiskerton further fuelled Parker's state of mind and by the time he returned home, he was *'maddened by drink and excitement.'*

At home, his mother had been anxiously waiting for her son to return. She seemed to have been expecting trouble as at about five o'clock, she had gone down the yard to the Spread Eagle public house to ask Mrs Doncaster, the landlady if Tom had gone there instead of returning home. Mrs Doncaster replied that she had not seen him and sensing that Mrs Parker was worried added, *'He will have a deal to tell you about what he saw in Sheffield."* "Yes," was the reply, "and perhaps there will be a deal to say to him," *evidently referring to the dissatisfaction felt by his father at his not having returned by the time stated. This was the foreshadowing of the dread event now so close at hand.'*

Mrs Doncaster was concerned enough to warn her husband, Cornelius, to *'keep out of the way lest he should sustain any injury in the quarrel which she expected between father and son.'* Mr Doncaster, described as a *'strong as well as a courageous and very temperate man,'* would often intervene, breaking up fights between Samuel and Tom, risking injury to himself on occasions, but more often than not, it was Tom who came off worst.

Mrs Parker returned down the yard to her own house and had begun to prepare tea with their servant girl, Hannah Burdon when young Parker arrived home. He was obviously drunk, and his mother asked him to sit down, but he just paced around the table and the house, at which point his father, Samuel, came in and asked him what he was going to do, commenting sharply that he had expected him home the night before to help get the seed corn in. As anticipated, an argument blew up with young Parker doubling his fists at his father and a great deal of shouting and swearing taking place.

Samuel was heard shouting, *'Go away, out of my house. I won't have you here. Get out, you rogue, you villain, you are a thief to me.'* Mrs Parker tried to get between them, shutting the door between the kitchen and the house place. Meanwhile, the servant girl ran out down the alleyway between Parker's house and next door to fetch their neighbour Mrs Haynes, who was also frequently called upon to act as peace-keeper between father and son. Hannah Burdon revealed later in her deposition that she stayed out in the street for about five minutes after fetching Mrs Haynes, as she dared not go back into the house. Later adding that she had never seen Parker double his fists at his father before, and neither had she been frightened of him before.

In the meantime, the fight had spilt out into the garden. The son struck at the father first, and then the father struck back, they gave blow for blow. The family were seen pushing and pulling at each other, with Mrs Parker continually trying to separate father and son, saying, *'Tom, you will not fight your father.'*

Mrs Haynes arrived on the scene and persuaded Samuel to go away and not say any more to his son. Young Parker walked off to the house, his mother followed him, whilst his father went into the stable. What was said in the house is not known, but Mrs Parker came back out and spoke to Mrs Haynes. She then returned to find out where her son was going and soon came back, making her way towards the pump in the garden, calling, *'Oh dear, he's got the gun and is going to shoot.'*

And shoot he did, both barrels straight through the glass in the windows in the direction of the stable where his father had gone. Various people heard the gunshots and hurried to the scene, Mrs Parker was on the floor by the pump, seemingly dead with the top part of her head blown off. It must have been horrific.

Mrs Haynes saw young Parker going down the yard and shouted to him, *'Oh Tom, you have shot your mother, you have shot her dead.'* He did not stop, and whilst Mrs Haynes was standing over his stricken mother, his father came out from the stable with blood pouring from his face saying to his son, *'What have you done it for?'* and Tom replied, *'You should not aggravate me so.'* Then, having left his hat on the table, he hurried off down the yard.

The whole tragic event from Parker's return home to the shooting had only taken between five and seven minutes.

Police Constable George Barksby, from the local station at Fiskerton, had been called by this time and accompanied by Samuel Foster, the local blacksmith and parish constable, went off in hot pursuit of Parker who had run off down the hauling path of the Trent. He had gone into the house of an old woman named Anne Birkett, where he fastened the door behind himself and pleaded with her to hide him, saying, *'Don't split, I have shot my mother dead.'*

He went towards the ladder that led to the upstairs and asked her to hide him. Mrs Birkett replied, saying, *'I have nowhere to put you.'* He repeated, *'I have shot my poor mother and shall be hanged.'* Mrs Birkett told him, *'I must get on with my work.'* Parker then went away.

This particular event was more passionately described by the rather expressive Nottinghamshire Guardian Supplement reporter as such: *'To render the narrative complete, we must now take it up at the point at which the fugitive, fresh from shedding the blood of a father and mother and with a curse deeper than that of Cain burning his brow and corroding his heart, left the cottage of the old woman Birkett, from whom, in helpless terror, he had sought an asylum, like some red-handed murderer of old flying to a convent for sanctuary.'*

After leaving Mrs Birkett's cottage, Parker continued down the path by the Trent and became aware that he had left his hat at home, he seemed concerned that being bare-headed might attract attention. By chance, a small boy came along, and Parker asked him to fetch his hat from the house. Meanwhile, Cornelius Doncaster had come up the yard with some brandy for Samuel Parker and noticed the gun on the side-board. He could see that both barrels had been fired.

When the boy arrived at the Parkers' house to enquire about the fugitive's hat, Mr Doncaster gave it to the boy and followed him towards where Tom Parker was *'waiting at Mr Allcock's lane end.'*

During this time, PC Barksby and Samuel Foster had searched for Parker in several yards and out-houses but then saw him on the Trent bank heading towards Newark. He did not seem to be in a hurry, evidently waiting for the boy to return with his hat. Barksby and Foster approached from different paths and eventually came across him *'leaning over a gate apparently in deep thought.'*

After a terrific struggle with Barksby, who was trying to handcuff him, Parker was eventually apprehended and charged with shooting his parents with the intent to murder them. He replied, *'I know all about it, I have done it, but it was purely accidental.'* He also asked, *'Is she seriously hurt?'* Parker was then escorted to Southwell lock up.

It had been intended for them to walk to Southwell, which would have taken over an hour, however, Parker refused but said if he must go, he would ride. Mr Allcock, a retired farmer, heard this and ordered his dog-cart to be brought out, but whilst this was being done, *'the prisoner turned again on Barksby and though handcuffed nearly succeeded in throwing him down.'* Eventually, Parker was put in the dog-cart, and they rode off to Southwell. On the way, he said, *'Do you think they will hang me?'* the policeman told him *'I don't know.'* Parker then replied, *'If they do, I will die on the scaffold like a b........dog.'* During the journey to Southwell, Parker sobered up a little to the consequences of his actions, and on arrival at the lock-up, he fainted twice. At the trial, PC Barksby stated that *'the prisoner was drunk, but not so bad but what he could walk.'*

In his deposition, Samuel Foster, when referring to Parker, stated that *'when in drink the son was a very passionate man.'* On this particular day, alas, he was beyond redemption.

Meanwhile, back in Fiskerton, poor Mrs Parker, who was miraculously still alive, had been carried into the house and lain on the sofa. A doctor was called for, and Mr Richard E. Cooke from Southwell attended her. Together with Mr Samuel Job from Newark, they were the two surgeons who cared for Mrs Parker throughout her ghastly ordeal.

Samuel Parker was very ill for a while, having received eleven shotgun pellets in his face and at least eight in his chest. He was so distraught at the thought of his son being in custody, that he could barely be kept in bed and begged for his son to be released so he could manage the farm. He made every excuse for him, blaming himself for provoking the argument, and it was thought that *'his condition still being very precarious it was considered advisable in the afternoon to send for a legal gentleman to make his will, and his inalienable partiality led him to leave all his property to the prisoner.'*

Samuel did make a full recovery physically, however, mentally, he suffered greatly. He later commented that his wounds were *'only like scratches of an old cat.'*

On Wednesday, the day after the shooting, Tom Parker was taken to Southwell House of Correction, where he was remanded for a week. On the 31st of March 1864, two days after the shooting, the prisoner was taken by cab back to Fiskerton, where depositions were being taken from the witnesses. These included his father, who in the presence of the prisoner and before both the Rev. T. C. Cane and the Honourable Col. Monkton, on his oath saith as follows:

[2]*'I live at Fiskerton and am a farmer. On Tuesday last, he came home rather groggy after 5 o'clock in the evening. He came in the house and I came in and scolded him. I thought he was got fresh and would have been better home. He was fresh. Me and his mother was in. I did not see the servant girl in. After I scolded him I went out of the house. My wife followed me out. I think he came out of the house and then went in again, but I am not sure, I mean my son when I say he. I have quite forgiven him.'*

PLAN OF THE CRIME SCENE

TOWN STREET

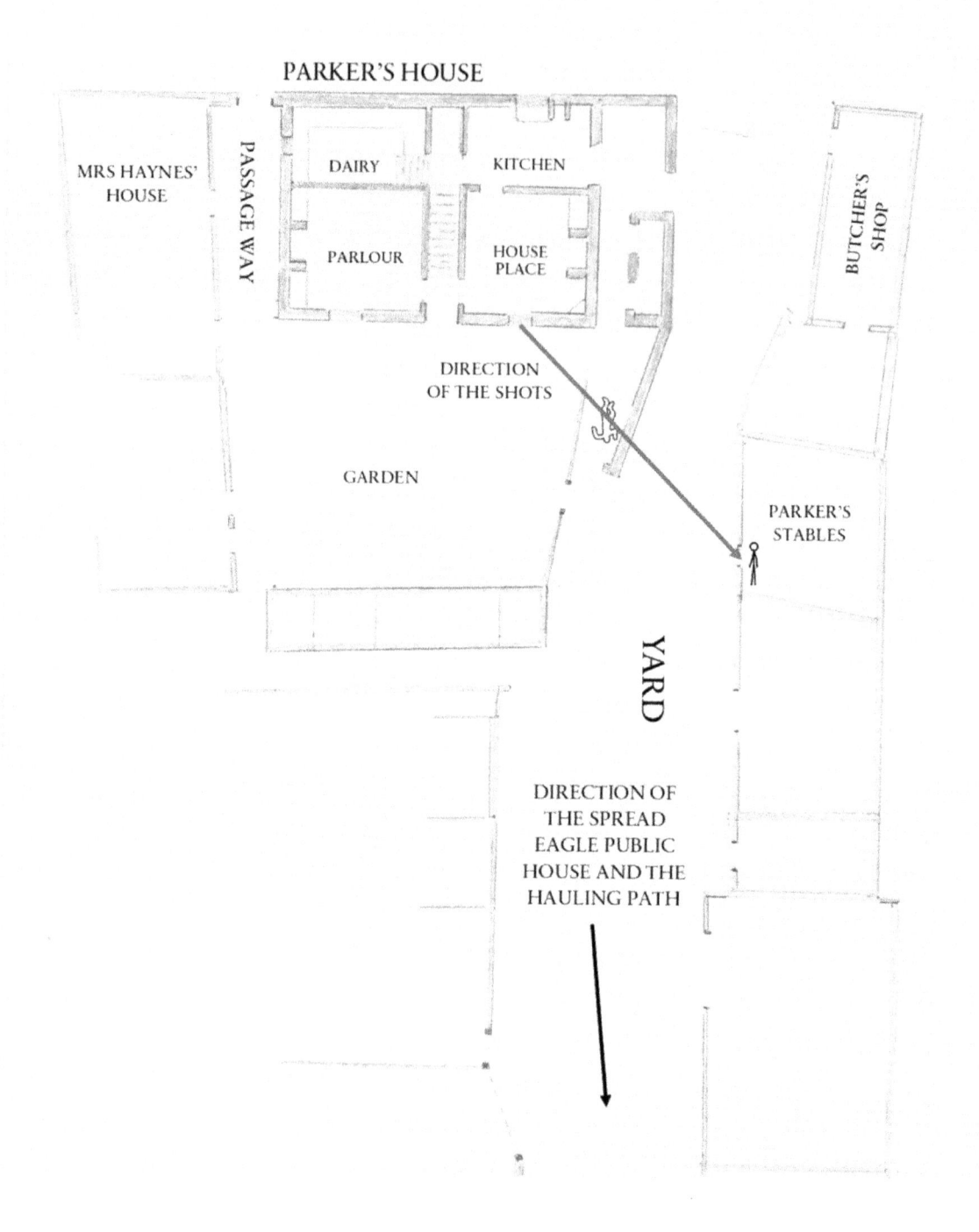

PARKER'S HOUSE

MRS HAYNES' HOUSE

PASSAGE WAY

DAIRY

KITCHEN

PARLOUR

HOUSE PLACE

BUTCHER'S SHOP

DIRECTION OF THE SHOTS

GARDEN

PARKER'S STABLES

YARD

DIRECTION OF THE SPREAD EAGLE PUBLIC HOUSE AND THE HAULING PATH

THE PETTY SESSIONS

Today's equivalent of Petty Sessions would be the Magistrates Court, and at noon on Saturday the 2nd of April 1864, Richard Thomas Parker was brought for examination before the Rev. T.C. Cane and the Hon. Colonel Monckton at the Petty Sessions Room, Southwell.

The shocking event of a few days earlier had been reported on the 1st of April 1864 in the Nottingham Guardian as:

'A DREADFUL OCCURRENCE AT FISKERTON.
FATHER AND MOTHER SHOT BY THEIR SON.'

The report outlined the terrible incident, and at this point, Parker would have been examined for the attempted murder of his parents. The case had attracted huge interest, and a large crowd had gathered in the streets, a body of which rushed to the Justice Room window in an effort to see the prisoner. Consequently, the magistrates decided to close the hearing to the public and press to prevent the case from being prejudged.

The prisoner's attorney, Mr Ashley, was able to observe the proceedings, and as young Parker entered the room, he appeared agitated and *'trembled perceptibly, but he ultimately recovered the equanimity he has generally displayed.'*

Various witnesses spoke to give their version of events, including Mrs Haynes, and it is her evidence that is the most interesting. Bear in mind that Mrs Parker was still alive at this stage in the proceedings and that she and Mrs Haynes were friends and neighbours and had been so for twenty years or more. The following are transcriptions of Mrs Haynes' evidence given at each of three separate petty sessions:

[3]*2 APRIL 1864*

MARY HAYNES upon her oath saith as follows:

I live at Fiskerton and am a widow. Tuesday night last the girl Hannah who was servant to Mr Parker (that girl there) came and fetched me. She said Master and Thomas was fighting and asked me to come, when I came I found them having a few words. Thomas and the mother were in the garden, and Mr Parker and me was standing by the hedge. Mr Parker and me was together one side of the hedge, and the other two were in

the garden. I was persuading Mr Parker to go away. Mr Parker went into the stable door, and Thomas went into the house and Mrs Parker followed him. Mistress then came out again at the same door. I was then standing against the wall in the yard, the big yard. I heard the report of a gun, but I don't know who shot it. I heard two reports. I went down to the end of the wall, and there Mrs Parker lay. Mr Foster and me took her indoors. She was bleeding. I sat her in a chair. When we picked her up she lay against the wall end.
   Signed
   Mary Haynes

9 APRIL 1864

MARY HAYNES upon her oath saith as follows:

Thomas whom I mentioned in my former deposition is the prisoner. When I heard the report of the gun, I was standing near the pump. I could not see into Mr Parker's house I <u>could not see the window</u>. I <u>could see over the wall</u>. I was standing between the small building and the pump. I never saw the smoke of the gun. I never saw the gun on Tuesday night. I was about three or four yards from Mrs Parker when she fell, but I did not see her fall. I saw her lying on the ground. Her head was in the yard. <u>She fell partly into the yard</u>. I believe I was the first person who saw her. I saw no one else about when I went to Mrs Parker to pick her up. Cope was the first that came after Mrs Parker fell, but he went away again. Mrs Parker had been out of the house about two or three minutes before I heard the report of the gun. Mr Samuel Foster was the first who helped pick her up. A great many people came when they heard the report of the gun. The gun was shot off when I was in the shade of the pump. I thought the row was all over and I was going up the wall side to go home. When I had got against the pump I heard the shots fired. When the first barrel was over I stood.
   Signed
   Mary Haynes

In each of these sworn statements, Mrs Haynes declares that she did <u>not</u> see Richard Thomas Parker in the house, nor did she see him fire the gun. However, at the third Petty Session, just over three weeks after the shooting had taken place, Mrs Haynes alters her deposition, declaring that she <u>did</u> see the accused at the window.

16 APRIL 1864

MARY HAYNES upon her oath saith as follows:

Before the shot was fired, I was against the wall end just below the pump. I was going home. I was just getting against the pump when the shot was fired. I saw Mr Thomas Parker (the prisoner) putting his coat on when I was against the wall end. I saw him through the <u>window of what they call the house-part</u>. When I saw him putting his coat on I went to go home and when I got against the pump the first shot was fired and I stood still. There was another shot, and I stood still for a few minutes, then I went to the end of the wall and saw Mrs Parker laying it might be a yard further down the yard than the pump. The first body I saw was John Cope and I asked him if he would help me up with her. I saw Mrs Parker come from the house as far as the pump. Master Parker, the father, opened the stable door and went as if he was going in but I cannot say whether he went in or not.

Signed
Mary Haynes

Richard Thomas Parker was detained in the County Gaol following the Petty Sessions, charged with shooting his parents with the intent to murder, and thus, committed for trial at the Assizes Court in Nottingham, now the National Justice Museum.

In the meantime, Mrs Parker had initially been making somewhat of a recovery at her home in Fiskerton. Her external wounds were healing well, she was able to talk and give directions about the farm and continued to ask for her son to be allowed home. She was also '*exceedingly reticent respecting admission that might criminate her son.*'

Sadly, about fourteen days after the shooting, she suffered a stroke leaving her paralysed down her left side, and from here on, she began to decline. If the Nottingham Guardian reporter was accurate with his dates, then Mrs Parker's stroke would have occurred <u>before</u> the 16th of April 1864 - the point at which Mrs Haynes changed her evidence. Perhaps with her friend's life hanging by a thread, she decided to tell the full version of the tragic events now that it looked very much like Mrs Parker might die.

Somehow though, she lingered on for several weeks being cared for by her friends and '*even in her latest mental wanderings, Mrs Parker occasionally broke out with the observation "I love Tom."* Sadly, she gradually began to decline, taking a turn for the worse on the 15th of May. She died at four minutes after 10 o'clock at night on the 16th of May 1864, forty-eight days after the shooting.

An offence so rank it smells to Heaven - A Mother's Murder!

A post-mortem was carried out by Messrs Edward Cooke and Samuel Job (Surgeons) on the 17th of May 1864, twenty-one hours after Mrs Parker's heartbreaking death that revealed '*the top part of her scalp had been blown off, laying the bone bare. There were several indentations in her forehead and corresponding perforations in her skull.*'

With no antibiotics available in the 19th century, infection set in, and the doctor's words at the trial were: '*The wounds produced inflammation and irritation which caused death.*' Followed by: '*I have not the least doubt that death was caused by the gunshot.*'

TRANSCRIPTION OF POST-MORTEM REPORT

[4]Post-mortem examination of the body of Mrs Parker, Fiskerton, 21 hours - after death on the 17th of May 1864.

<u>External Appearances</u>

A wound 3 inches square on the vertex of the head exposing the outer table of the skull which the process of nature is separating from the rest of the bone this wound is cicatrizing at the edges 3 or 4 scars such as would be occasioned by shot having passed thro' the scalp are noticed on the right side of the forehead. No other mark or injury to be found on any part of the body.

On removing the scalp patches of effused blood were found over the forehead and left temporal region. Over the right side of the frontal and anterior part of right parietal bones from 12-15 indentations and holes from shot were seen in 3 or 4 places the shot was sticking in the outer table of the skull & I pick'd two or three out with the fingers (these shot with me I found lying loose between the dura mater and internal table of the skull in the interior of the head I gave to Mr Cooke's assistant to take care of) In the other places the shot had struck very close together and appeared to have driven portions of bone into the interior of the skull.

<u>Internal Appearances</u>

On opening the head about 2 ounces of matter mixed with blood was found beneath the dura mater at the apex of the brain, the vessels of the internal membrane pia mater were very much congested & patches of matter were found over the surface of the brain in various places - the brain itself was of a much darker colour and very much softer than normal - on slicing it up a quantity of matter was found in the right ventricle, not any in the left ventricle.

No coagulum of any description could be found in any part of the brain. The paralysis in life was in my opinion caused by the abscess beneath the membranes of the apex of the brain. No shot could be found in the interior of the brain - although the fact of the matter being found in the right ventricle & of there having been one complete perforation thro' the skull would favour the idea of one having passed in that direction.

<u>Skull Cap</u>

On its internal surface present 4 or 5 prominences and a hole sufficiently large to admit the point of the little finger. These prominences correspond to the shot marks described externally on the right frontal and parietal bones-the shots shattered the internal table of the skull and caused portions of bone to press upon the membranes of the brain - The irritation set-up by these spicula of bone would be very likely to cause severe inflammation of the brain and its membranes. The result of which inflammation would be the abscess already described.

At the request of the Coroner, I brought away the portion of the skull containing these injuries and have in my possession. I believe the cause of death to have been an abscess of the brain the result of a slow inflammation of the brain set up by the injuries received.

<u>Body</u>

An examination was made of the rest of the body, but the other viscera were found perfectly healthy.

On the morning of the 18th of May, Superintendent Bexon called upon me stating that Mr Cook's assistant had gone away and taken the shot with him I had given to him the night before. At Superint't Bexon's request, I took out 2 more shot from the skull in my possession one from the outside and the other from the inside these were pick'd out with a penknife & given to Bexon, my assistant Mr Johnson being present at the time.

Post-mortem kindly transcribed by Dr Alan Stevens

Illustration of the inside of Mrs Parker's skull

Complete perforation

Illustration of the outside of Mrs Parker's skull as seen at the post-mortem, showing the complete and incomplete perforations

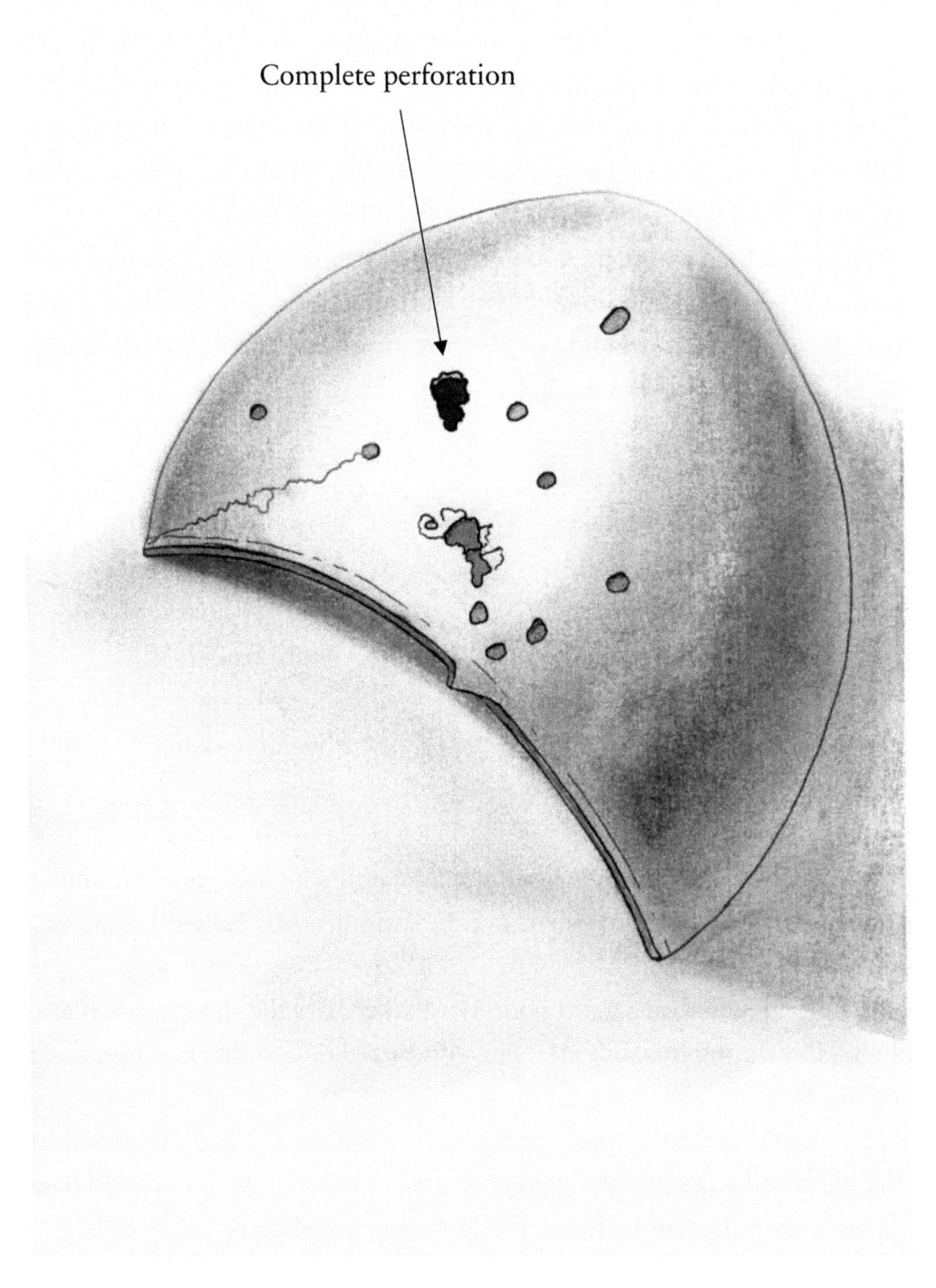

Complete perforation

THE INQUEST

During this period of history, inquests were invariably carried out in public houses with the body of the deceased lain out for all to see, and Mrs Parker's was no exception. Following the post-mortem, the initial inquest hearing took place on Tuesday the 17th of May 1864 at the Spread Eagle Inn, home of Mr Cornelius Doncaster, situated at the opposite end of the yard from where the shooting took place. The proceedings were held before Mr William Newton, Gentleman - Coroner and read:

[5]'An Inquisition then and there taken on view of the body of the said Elizabeth Parker then and there lying dead as follows to wit:' The inquest was then adjourned until seven o'clock on the Saturday morning. The following jurors were 'bound in the sum of £20 to appear.'

Gervas Wright	John Clark
George Whitaker	Edward Barker
John Miller	Thomas Pacey
Edward Driver	Henry Arnold
John May	John Arnold
John Esam	John Clark
William Wright	Edward Barker
Richard Jenkinson	

Various witnesses were called, including John Cope, who had overheard the fight and the gunshots, but when asked to help move the wounded Mrs Parker, he refused, saying he felt ill and too frightened.

Jane Richmond, who had nursed poor Mrs Parker after the shooting, was also called and unbelievably during this time, Mrs Parker declared to Jane that her injuries had been sustained in a fall.

Items belonging to Mrs Parker, including her shawl, cap and handkerchief, were produced, these were *'perforated with shot and showed marks of blood.'* It was also reported that some false hair had been found in the coal-place.

From other statements, it was understood that the gun belonged to Tom Parker, but Samuel had loaded it a few days before on Good Friday to *'shoot the crows and sparrows among the peas,'* however, the gun had not been discharged.

When sixty-two-year-old Samuel made his statement at the inquest, he refused to say anything against his son, expressing that he blamed himself very much for what had happened, wishing so much that he had not provoked the fatal argument.

The Nottinghamshire Guardian reported Samuel Parker's testimony as follows:

'No man in the world could say that he saw my son use the gun. No one could see into my house. I did not take particular notice of the powder, shot and bag produced, but I have seen them about the house. I did not see the gun in the house that day. I went to the stable to look after my horses. I cannot remember how I was shot myself. I did not know that I was shot. No one could swear that my son shot me unless by false swearing.

The Coroner: Did not Mrs Parker say to you 'get out of the way, Tom had got a gun.'- I never heard her mention that. I will swear it. I declare I never heard her mention it.

I would rather put down no evidence at all than not put down the truth - you did not hear your wife say that? - I am very dull of hearing. I did not hear her; I did not hear the barrels go off.

Your son had asked your leave to go to Sheffield and you refused it? - I told him it would be as good if he would stay at home and help me get my seed in but we had no words.

Did you not refuse to let him have any money? - No. He did not ask me. He had money of his own. He never asked me for any money at all.

He did not come home on the Monday night? - No sir. He did not come that night, but he did on Tuesday evening and he was very fresh. I was not aware that he was so fresh, or I should not have said a word to him. I blame myself very much.

I believe that you had a round or two with him? - Sir?

He stripped to fight you? - I do not know that he did. He came at me. I do not know how it was. I forget.

Were not you sparring a bit? - I am sure I do not know. I had no business to say anything to him when he was so very fresh. I blame myself.

Did you hit him? - I do not know. I may have done so. I was very angry for him being so tipsy. There would not have been anything of it if I had said nothing to him. I am very sorry it has happened. It is a bad job for me.

What did you do then? Did Mrs Parker put him one way and you the other? - *I am sure I forget.*

Did she part you? - *I am sure, sir, I do not know.*

You are sure you did not hear her say 'Tom has got the gun?' - *I never heard her I am sure, but he went to the house and I went to the stables.*

You remember no more? - *I do not remember any more.*

You were injured in the face? - *Yes. I had some scratches as if an old cat had scratched me.*

Was your coat shot through? - *I cannot say that it was.*

Did you not see some shot marks on the stable door? - *I cannot say that I did and I do not want to. It is no credit to me.*

Coroner (to Mr Wright): Do you, Mr Foreman, or the gentlemen of the jury wish to ask anything more?

Mr Wright: No; it is of no use.

Witness: I have no more to say; it would never have happened if I had not said something to him if I had kept out of the house.'

A further point to consider before committing Richard Thomas Parker to trial is the evidence given by Mrs Haynes. After changing her story at the third Petty Session, at the inquest, she elaborated further stating that: *'Just before the shots were fired I saw the son Thomas Parker against the window in the front room and almost immediately after I saw him put his coat on, I saw him with the gun in his hand. I saw him put it to his shoulder and point it in the direction of the deceased. I was about a yard or two from Mrs Parker and slipt round the wall corner and instantly the shot was fired.'*

[I have no doubt the son Richard Thomas Parker from what I saw fired the shot]
An incriminating statement for sure.

She also commented that Tom was *'tipsy, he was not so fresh as that he could not go or stand; but he was very fresh, he could walk. I believe he was very drunk.'*

Despite his father's pleas, a verdict of Wilful Murder was returned against Richard Thomas Parker, and he was committed for trial on the coroner's warrant. The whole proceedings had taken seven hours, with the jury coming to their conclusion in only ten minutes.

THE TRIAL

The trial took place at the County Court on Monday the 25th of July 1864 before Mr Justice (Colin) Blackburn. The galleries were crowded mainly with women who seemed to have taken the case to heart. Barristers for the prosecution were Mr George Boden QC and Mr Samuel Bristowe, and the delicate task of defending Richard Thomas Parker had fallen upon Mr Sergeant O'Brien, who was instructed by Mr Ashley, Parker's solicitor from Newark. The names of the sworn jurors were as follows:

Messrs. W Harrison (foreman)	John Watson
Thomas Spittlehouse	William Beeston
John Hill	Matthew Peck
B Beardsall	William Widdowson
Samuel Clayton	Elijah Brumpton
John Lillyman	George Beilby

As Parker lay in the County Gaol awaiting trial, he was described as being '*cheerful and animated,*' never expecting to be found guilty of wilful murder, and his instructions to Mr Ashley, his solicitor, were directed in the belief that he had not intended to hurt either of his parents.

Thus, Parker was brought before the court. He was dressed in a '*suit of black, with a frock and velvet collar.*' The Nottingham Journal reporter describes the prisoner as being a middle-sized man wearing moustaches and whiskers of a light colour. His coverage of the execution gives a slightly more colourful description when the reporter adds: '*He presented the appearance of a well built, good looking young man, though there was a sinister look about his keen grey eye.*'

Parker was then indicted with: '*the wilful murder of his mother Elizabeth Parker on the 16 May 1864. He was further indicted for feloniously shooting at Elizabeth Parker on the 29 March 1864 with the intent to murder her and further with feloniously shooting at Samuel Parker with intent to murder him on the 29 March. He was also charged with wilful murder on the coroner's warrant.*'

To each of these charges, he pleaded not guilty, and although he spoke in a firm voice, he outwardly showed signs of understanding the seriousness of his felony, and at the mention of his poor dead mother, Parker's eyes filled with tears.

A written copy of the charge against him contains the following powerful phrases, [6]*'that Richard Thomas Parker, late of the township of Fiskerton in the County of Nottingham not having the fear of God before his eyes but being moved and seduced by the instigation of the devil...'*

It continues with such phrases as *'feloniously wilfully and of his malice aforethought did make an assault...* And so on and so forth.

Each of the witnesses gave their statements relating their account of the terrible event. A 19th-century forensic investigation had been undertaken, with plans of the Parkers' house and garden at Fiskerton presented to the jury. Detailed measurements and calculations of the crime scene were taken to ascertain whether Parker was telling the truth when he alleged that he did not see either of his parents when he fired the gun.

Mr John Jackson, the engineer and architect who drew up the plans, was examined by Mr Bristowe for the prosecution, he said:

'I made the plan produced. It is an accurate plan of Mr Parker's premises at Fiskerton. I took the height of the walls. The height of the wall near the pump is four feet from the ground. The privet hedge, when measured by me, was rather under four feet. I saw two panes broken in the house window. The height from the floor to the centre of the panes is 4 feet 9 inches. The height of the pane outside is 4 feet 7 inches. The distance from the window to the wall is 17 feet and the distance from the window to the centre of the stable door 44 feet. The ground drops 16 inches from the window to the stable door. A person standing at the window can see the stable door. If a person stood at the house window with a gun, the line of fire would be beyond the corner of the wall. Some shots might touch the wall. — (By Mr O'Brien): To break a pane of glass by each shot would require the person to stand close to the window. The room is 7 feet by 12. There are eight squares of glass in the window and two sashes.'

Mr Sergeant O'Brien, for the defence, made a valiant attempt at trying to reduce the charge against Parker to manslaughter, with pleas that the defendant was far more susceptible to the evils of drink since his accident a few years before when he fell from a horse and received head injuries.

He suggested that after the argument between father and son, young Parker went back into the house, not with the intent of picking up the gun and shooting his father but only to put on his coat to go out. It was in a flash of anger that he seized the gun and fired the fatal shots. Mr O'Brien even tried for the sympathy vote by implying that as an only child, Parker would have been much loved by his mother, making it unlikely that he would ever have wanted to harm her.

As Mr O'Brien *'with fervid passages'* addressed the court and implored the jury to consider whether the facts *'point to a deliberate, well-formed and settled purpose of mind or whether they lead to the conclusion of a reckless, wanton, impulse of the moment,'* the prisoner *'flushed considerably and perspiration exuded from his forehead and he shifted his place from the middle of the dock rail to the corner of the dock nearest to the learned counsel.'*

Although the law at this time did not allow an accused person to give sworn evidence in their own defence, they were entitled to give an unsworn statement to the jury that was not subject to cross-examination as a way of expressing their version of events. Parker would have had this right, but for some unknown reason, he either chose not to or was instructed by his defence not to speak on his own behalf.

On a similar note, no witnesses were called by the defence, even though Parker's friend, Mr Daybell, was waiting outside the court ready to speak up for him. In a letter Parker wrote to Daybell after the trial, he commented that he felt *'assured that you would have done your best for me and I feel also assured, had my counsel called for witnesses to speak to my treatment of my parents, it would have very much altered the aspect of the case, for the judge took a very wrong opinion of it.'*

Again, it is unknown why the witness was not called unless it was felt he could have done more harm than good. Perhaps Mr Daybell was deemed an unreliable witness, for in the same letter, Parker did ask of Daybell to *'Give my love to all enquiring friends and particularly to R. Swinscoe. Tell him I often think about him. Tell him to alter his course of life and give his heart to God and he will never repent it as long as he lives.'*

And so, Mr Justice Blackburn summed up the evidence to the jury. He said, *'the charge was one of great magnitude and one that required careful consideration.'* He added that they must look at the evidence and decide *'as to the intention with which the shot was fired.'*

They were to consider whether Parker's intentions were *'such as in their opinion to make the crime one of wilful murder or manslaughter, or whether it was possible that under the circumstances there was no crime committed at all, but that the shooting of the prisoner's father and mother was as the prisoner had said, purely accidental.'*

Despite the defence's noble efforts, his argument won Parker no favours, and the jurors retired. Verdicts were drawn up much quicker in the past than in today's courtrooms. Often the jurors never left the court to deliberate the case, but the jury in Parker's case was out for about an hour, which was actually quite a long time.

And so, at half-past three, a verdict was returned of:

'GUILTY of WILFUL MURDER but recommend him mercy because he was in liquor.'

Mr Justice Blackburn then asked the prisoner why sentence of death should not be passed upon him, and he replied, *'I had no intention to do it. I fired the shot with no intention at all. I had no intention to hit them. I never saw either parties when I fired the shot.'*

With that, the judge donned his black cap and passed sentence to Parker that he be: *'taken from the place in which you now stand to the prison from which you came, and that, on a day to be named, you be taken to the place of execution and hanged by the neck till you are dead, and that your body be taken down and buried in the precincts of the prison in which you shall have last been confined, and may God have mercy on your soul.'*

On hearing his sentence passed, Parker appeared to show no sign of emotion, and due to an error in the court proceedings, the many women who came to witness the trial were accidentally excluded, leaving the room with *'scarcely any visible signs of feeling among the audience.'* The prisoner was then led from the dock. He later said that *'his counsel did not cross-examine the witnesses sufficiently, but that was a mistaken notion, it being impossible to shake in the least the facts as stated in evidence.'* The most tragic part of the trial was the fact that Parker's father was present. After hearing his son sentenced to die, he left the court being carried away by friends in a state of semi-stupefaction and went into the street. *'Here he was surrounded by a mob of persons, who followed the old man down the Pavement and compelled him to take refuge in one of the buildings near the Town Hall.'*

How utterly heartbreaking it must have been for him.

EFFORTS TO GAIN A REPRIEVE

The date for the execution was set for the morning of Wednesday the 10th of August 1864, and Messrs. Clarke, Rothera and Carter, solicitors of Nottingham, were employed by *'Parker's friends'* to draw up three petitions for people to sign on Parker's behalf. Nearly all the people of Fiskerton and Rolleston signed, and in Newark, about 170 signatures were obtained, although it was felt that more people would have signed if the wording of the letter had been different. It required that the petitioners must have known the prisoner for some years before his accident when he fell from the horse some seven years ago. Unfortunately, in Newark, relatively few had known him during that time. Together though, a surprisingly large amount of people signed as they all *'generally entertained the opinion that the convict did not really intend to kill his mother.'*

On the Friday before the fated day, Parker's solicitor Mr Ashley, travelled to London to meet with Mr Waddington, the Under Secretary of State. He went through the depositions and any additional information that Mr Ashley had been able to muster in Parker's favour, including the signed petitions that had already been forwarded to London. It was hoped Mr Waddington could be convinced that there had been no *'malicious intention'* and consider the information *'sufficiently strong to warrant a commutation of the sentence to transportation for life.'*

The reply received on the Sunday was not favourable, it read:

Whitehall, 6th August 1864

Gentlemen, I am directed by Secretary Sir George Grey to acknowledge the receipt of your letter, forwarding three petitions on behalf of Richard Thomas Parker, now under sentence of death for murder and I am to acquaint you that after careful consideration of all the facts of the case, Sir George Grey regrets that he can see no grounds to justify him in advising Her Majesty to interfere with the due course of the law. I am, gentlemen, your obedient servant,
H. WADDINGTON
Under Secretary of State for the Home Department.

Not to be deterred by this response, the solicitors held a meeting on the Sunday evening with the Rev. William Howard, chaplain of the County Gaol, and it was decided to send a telegram to Mr Waddington to ask if Sir George Grey would receive a deputation. By return telegraph, they were informed that he had now left town to go to his country seat in Falloden, Chathill, Northumberland and that they should telegraph him there directly.

This was duly done, however, the reply received seemed hopeless *'as Mr Waddington has seen the solicitor and given him a final answer, it is useless for Sir G. Grey to receive a deputation.'*

Still resolute, another letter was dispatched to Sir George Grey on Monday night in the form of a memorial, fully outlining the circumstances of the tragic shooting and the unfortunate events leading up to that fateful evening. It also highlighted the rather curious matter of Mrs Haynes's evidence.

As previously mentioned, in her first two depositions at the Southwell Petty Sessions, she stated that she did <u>not</u> see Parker at the window before he fired the gun. However, from then on, she always maintained that she had seen Parker putting his coat on, then put the gun to his shoulder and point it in the direction of his mother. The letter continued to suggest that Mrs Haynes's change in statement had been based on *'mere imagination'* thus *'in the absence, therefore of Mrs Haynes's evidence, there was no proof whatever that the prisoner intended to shoot either his father or his mother. The catastrophe might therefore have been the result of an indiscreet but not criminal act on his part.*

A copy of the letter was also sent to Mr Waddington along with the following communication:

To H. Waddington, Esq., Under Secretary of State for the Home Department.
Re THOMAS PARKER

Sir - We telegraphed to Sir George Grey immediately on the receipt of your telegram this morning and in reply received from Sir George Grey the following: "As Mr Waddington has seen the solicitor and given him a final answer, it is useless for Sir G. Grey to receive a deputation." We have this evening written Sir George a statement of which we beg to enclose you a copy and have forwarded him a petition of which we also enclose you a copy. If you feel with us that there are circumstances in this case which may fairly justify a respite or commutation of the sentence passed upon the unhappy convict, we beg that you will immediately communicate with Sir George by telegraph. You are, of course aware that the execution is fixed for Wednesday morning.

With thanks for your prompt attention hitherto, we are sir, your obedient servants.

CLARKE, ROTHERA AND CARTER
Nottingham, 8th Aug 1864

It was believed no reply to this final plea was received, and whether Mrs Haynes saw Parker with the gun or not, one has to ask oneself, would it have made any difference to the final, fatal outcome?

It was probably more unfortunate that only a few months before Parker's foul deed, a man named George Victor Townley had been convicted of murder in Derby and sentenced to hang. However, he was reprieved at the last moment on the grounds of insanity. He came from an upper-middle-class family who used influence over the same Sir George Grey and whose solicitor took advantage of a sloppy law relating to insanity, *'Further Provision for the Confinement and Maintenance of Insane People - 3 & 4 Victoria, c. 54.'* There was public outrage over the decision on the basis that a poor man would not have received the same reprieve, and the law was changed. Townley, in the meantime, now committed to an asylum, killed himself by jumping over a staircase railing landing on his head upon a stone floor, twenty-three feet below.

This case might have swayed the decision of a reprieve for Parker, rightly or wrongly, and the crowd at Parker's hanging were heard chanting Townley's name, in the widespread belief that as Townley had escaped the death penalty, they felt Parker should also have been reprieved.

THE END IS NIGH

Richard Thomas Parker's last days in prison are described in detail in the newspapers. Two guards watched over him day and night, and it would seem he found refuge with God, attending the prison chapel and receiving visits from Mr Attenborough, a Methodist Minister from Newark. The report also contains intimate letters written to his estranged wife and others to his friends, pleading with them to visit him once more before he is executed, urging them to mend their ways and travel a clean and sober path henceforward. Copious prayers for forgiveness were uttered, but one might be forgiven for thinking it might be a bit too late now.

Many tears were shed by the prisoner during these visits, and to his aunts, he expressed deep remorse for bringing shame and disgrace upon the family.

On the Monday, two days before Parker's execution, he was visited by his father and his estranged wife, Emily, accompanied by her brother-in-law, Mr Abbott, and her two children. She wished very much for eighteen-month-old Samuel to say farewell to his father, but she was dissuaded by the family from doing so. They were met at the train station by Samuel's brother, Thomas, and the group walked up to the County Gaol. By some considerable misfortune, they arrived at the same moment the drop was being carried towards the lobby, only a short distance from where it was to be fixed for the execution.

When Emily visited her condemned husband, despite everything that had happened between them, '*they literally flew into each other's embrace with arms locked round each other's neck and remained in that position during the whole of the interview.*'

Between sobs, Parker confessed that he wished he had taken his wife's advice as he would not now be in this tragic position.

The Guardian reporter again poetically added, '*How can we attempt to paint the harrowing anguish of soul-the intense grief of those two young people, who, if all had been well, might have lived in the enjoyment to the highest connubial felicity?*'

Parker told his wife that if she would like a portrait of him, the governor would take one for her, but she replied that she already had one. The visit lasted about three-quarters of an hour, after which '*the interview closed in the most painful and agonising manner—*

the parties having eventually to be separated from each other.' It was reported that Parker was very shaken up for several hours after the visit, *'but afterwards recovered his usual composure.'*

Samuel Parker's visit was the most heart-rending, he had threatened to kill himself on the day if his son was hanged and had to be observed carefully by the police and family. *'The appearance of the old man was careworn in the extreme and in his face, the lines of grief were deeply graven.'* There were shot wound marks on his face and chest, where pellets were still embedded. The reporter described him thus: *'the old man apparently feeling more poignant anguish than if he had been in the criminal's place, from the consciousness that he entertains of the harshness of his manner to his son having so greatly contributed to the sad and fatal deed.'*

As news arrived at the prison that there was to be no reprieve, *'the old man was told that all hope for his son's life was over, the only answer he made was, "My poor lad."* When father and son met in the prison cell, both were so distraught that neither could speak, and it was suggested by the chaplain that Samuel come back in a few minutes once he had recovered some of his composure. Eventually, they were able to talk, however, *'No reference was at any time made to the commission of the act - excepting by the prisoner, who said at the time he fired the shots he did not see either his father or his mother and that he had no intention of killing either of them. It was a fit of passion.'*

Poor Samuel must have carried the weight of the whole sordid affair with him for the next twenty years until his death in 1884.

Following these distressing visits, it was decided that no other visitors should be allowed as Parker had become extremely upset and now only wished to prepare for his fate. Several of his relations were denied admittance from then on.

In the meantime, as Samuel and Emily attempted to leave the prison, they unfortunately fell victim to Victorian 'celebrity spotters.' A huge crowd had gathered, making it impossible for them to leave by the usual entrance. The prison governor made arrangements for them to use a private door but even then, as Emily's brother-in-law went for a cab, *'the crowd observed the cab drive up to another door and instantly there was a rush to obtain a sight of Mrs Parker. The horse's head was seized by the mob, and it was not until a strong body of police had been sent for that they could be dispersed.'*

All that remained now was for the gallows to be erected on the front steps of the

County Gaol. The work carried on through Tuesday night, and '*the heavy clanking noise of their hammers reverberated on the midnight air with an awful sound, which might be distinctly heard by the wretched man whose life was so fast drawing to a close.*'

Transcription of one of the letters Parker wrote to his wife, Emily:

From the COUNTY GAOL

2nd of AUGUST 1864

My dear wife - While I am writing these few lines to you I feel such a feeling of love for you and the dear children that I can scarcely express myself in words to you. Oh, that I could redeem the past! What a life of happiness would we lead. Would that God had given me the same hope and feelings when I had my liberty as he has given me now. How happy might we have been. If you think I have been happy without you, you are sadly mistaken. You have always been uppermost in my thoughts. Many is the time that I have come over to Newark since you left me, hoping to see you, if only at a distance. You may guess my feelings when I have not been able to do so. It has often driven me to drinking and to such a state of recklessness, that I have done things that in my sober moments I could not have thought possible. You have no doubt thought I cared nothing about you when you have seen me (which no doubt you have done) but you must not take everyone by their looks, or you may be deceived, for under many a smiling countenance the heart lies sad within. But it is all over now - for the die is cast. I have almost lost all hope of seeing you in this world, but I hope we shall soon meet again in heaven, where I shall be ready to welcome you to eternal happiness and glory. Oh, what a happy meeting that will be. Try my dear Pem to obtain God's forgiveness and mercy and bring up the dear children in the fear of the Lord. Warn Sam [meaning his little son] of drinking and gambling. Tell him of his father's fate that it may be a warning to him. God bless you all. I should so like to see you I hope you will not deny me that pleasure but come over as soon as you can. Write by return and believe me your ever-loving husband,

R.T. PARKER.

THE EXECUTION

Preparations for the execution commenced on Monday the 8th of August 1864, at six o'clock in the morning, and were supervised by Mr R.C. Sutton, the architect. The excavations were carried out by Mr Thumb, and Messrs. Thomas Hall and Sons took care of the joinery. Barriers were to be erected to control the crowd so there would not be a repeat of the deaths and injuries sustained at the hanging of [7]William Saville, twenty years previously, in 1844.

1861 SALMON'S MAP OF NOTTINGHAM

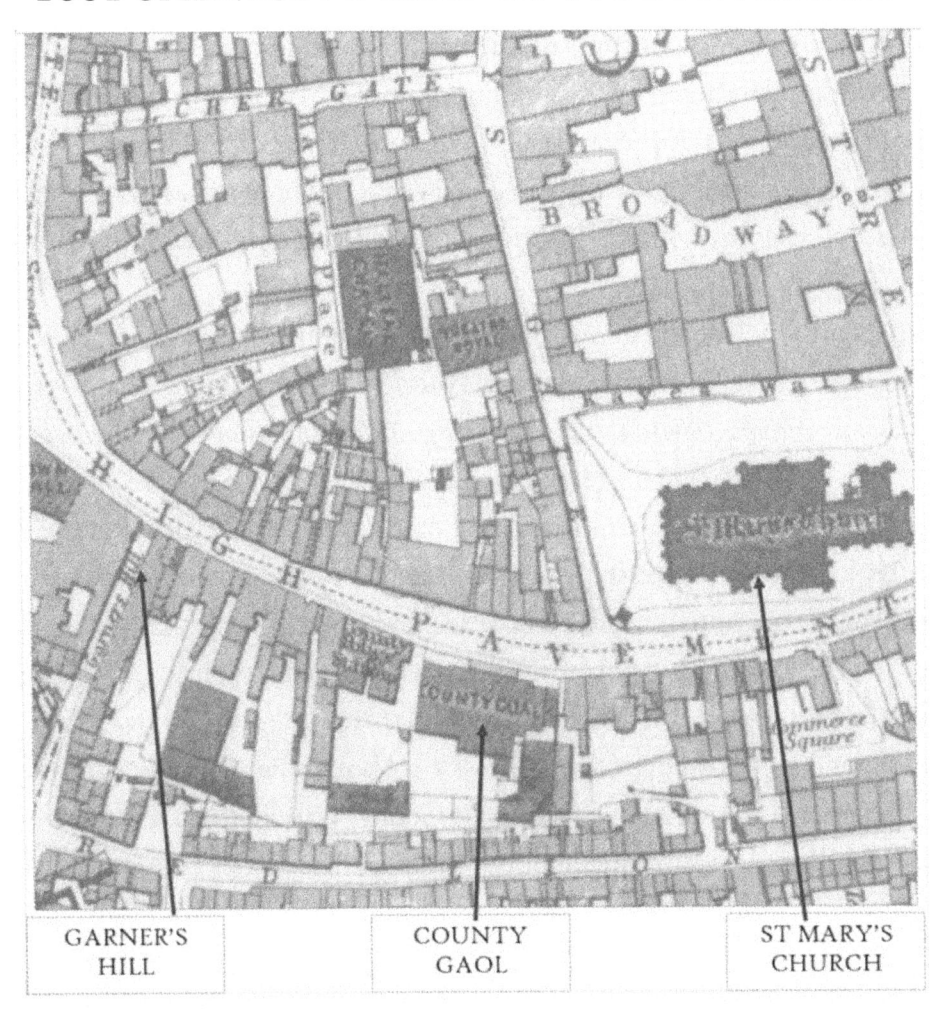

| GARNER'S HILL | COUNTY GAOL | ST MARY'S CHURCH |

During Saville's execution, the crowd had become agitated, and as people panicked, they were crushed against the buildings on High Pavement. Many ran towards Garner's Hill, some tripped and fell, and bodies began to pile up, creating a bottleneck. People were dying and sustaining terrible injuries. In all, twelve were killed in the crush, five more died later, numerous more were seriously injured, and out of the dead, eight were under the age of fifteen.

Barricades were built in front of the County Gaol railings, six other barriers were completed along the street leading up towards Weekday Cross and a further six in the opposite direction towards St Mary's Church. The design effectively separated the crowd into two sections which were then subdivided into additional smaller divisions, thus preventing anyone from being crushed. The entrances and exits were diagonally opposite each other, and a person would have to zig-zag through the six barriers to walk towards the scaffold. As a further precaution, the lower storey windows in houses along High Pavement were either shuttered or boarded up against pressure from the crowd.

The scaffold was erected at the front of the County Gaol directly over the entrance, '*the drop being on a level with the upper part of the lintel of the door-way, the unhappy man would hang down to within a short distance of the steps leading to the entrance hall.*'

About fifty county police and about eighty borough police maintained order, and the newspaper reported that '*No arrangements could have been more complete and no precaution that could be devised for preserving order and guarding against accident neglected.*'

Inside the gaol, every care was being undertaken to '*alleviate the agony*' of the doomed prisoner, to which Parker expressed his gratitude. Two keepers and a sheriff's officer accompanied Parker continually, and he now seemed resigned to his fate.

On the eve of the fateful day of execution, Parker received the Holy Communion, the Rev. W. Howard declared he was satisfied that Parker was in '*a proper state of mind*' and one of his uncles was allowed to visit him for a short while. In the meantime, the executioner, Thomas Askerne, had arrived at the County Gaol in a cab. He was unnoticed by the crowd that had already gathered outside to watch the barriers and scaffold being erected.

And so, dawn broke on Wednesday the 10th of August 1864, the day of the execution.

Some rain had fallen in the night, and the air was cool, clouds began to build up, and although more rain was expected, it did remain dry. It was suggested that about 10,000 people were gathered, many of them having been there all night, although that number might be somewhat exaggerated.

People from all classes of society came to witness the hanging, the Guardian reporter wrote that *'persons of tender and sympathetic organization, who shudder even at a cut finger and would hesitate to kill a chicken, feel interested in seeing a fellow being choked to death by the prescribed but barbarous mode which the law of this realm only allows.'*

He then commented that *'by far the greater proportion of the crowd were evidently possessed of a very low mental organisation and the dull, morose expression of countenance, which usually characterises a great portion of such crowds, was on this occasion especially observable.'*

The atmosphere was more a celebration than a hanging, as was the case at all public executions. The crowd occupied themselves with such antics as *'bonneting'* much to the annoyance of the ladies having their bonnets tapped. And whenever a crinoline collapsed, there was much amusement, especially when a man held up a crinoline hoop in the shape of a noose. Mock fights broke out here and there, and various persons held poles with religious scripts written on them such as *"Eternity is near", "Behold the Lamb of God",* and *"Jesus only."*

However, apart from some raucous behaviour amongst the *'roughs'* in the crowd, the authorities congratulated themselves that no serious incidents or accidents occurred.

And so, the doomed Richard Thomas Parker had woken early after about three hours sleep. He dressed in his own clothes, *'a suit of dark tweed'*, then spent time praying and writing a last letter to his wife. He ate breakfast at six o'clock, after which he prayed further and *'appeared to be a thoroughly converted man and a sincere believer in the saving truths of Christianity. He talked with resigned composure to the two men left in charge of him and bade them an affectionate farewell.'*

At a quarter to eight, the prison governor arrived and handed Parker over to the custody of the sheriff's representatives. A funeral procession was formed, and they made their way to the pinioning room, where Parker was to meet his executioner for the first time. Askerne was described as *'a tall, muscular man with bushy black whiskers, streaked with grey'* and *'the beau ideal of his profession.'*

The chaplain read the 51st Psalm to which Parker fervently joined in, whilst his arms were deftly pinioned with a leather belt. The governor then asked him if he wished to say any last words. '*The wretched man, in a firm and audible, but subdued voice said:- I beg to return my grateful thanks to all the parties who have taken any share in the attempts to get me reprieved. It was very kind in them to try to spare my life. But I am resigned to die. I know I have acted very wrongly, but I never intended to do this deed. I never intended to shoot either my father or my mother. Far from it. I never saw either of them at the time. But I did fire the gun and I am sorry for it.*'

At 8 o'clock in the morning, the scene was set. The procession now reformed, was led out from the gaol, and as Parker stepped up onto the scaffold, he began praying silently to himself. He stood firmly, looking '*haggard and nervous,*' as the hangman put on the white cap, adjusted the noose and retired to draw the bolt. The chaplain read the words, '*Man that is born of a woman hath but a short time to live and is full of misery. He cometh up and he is cut down like a flower, he fleeth as it were a shadow and never continueth in one stay.*' Parker's hands '*twitched nervously, turning a blue colour whilst his breath came in long gasps*' as the chaplain continued with the words, '*In the midst of life we are in death.*'

The bolt was drawn with a terrible sound... '*The culprit meanwhile gave several convulsive quivers, and after some struggles which lasted rather longer than usual, his soul was launched into eternity.*' It was widely agreed amongst many that Parker died hard and as the newspaper reporter so eloquently put it: '*Thus, finished the career of a young man in the prime of life, of good intellect, connections and prospects, all made worthless by an indulgence in the passions which wrought his ruin.*'

His body was left hanging on the gallows for an hour, it was then cut down and buried within the precincts of the gaol. A few hours later, Askerne was '*sitting in the bar of the County Tavern quietly smoking a cigar.*'

Richard Thomas Parker was the last man to be publicly hanged in Nottingham. The last public execution in Britain took place in 1868 outside Newgate Prison, London.

Although Parker would probably still be charged with murder in a present-day trial, the question today is whether a jury might only convict him of manslaughter. Fire the gun he most certainly did, and the shot that hit his mother caused her death, of that there is no doubt. But was this a premeditated decision taken when Parker returned to the house following the fight with his father? Or a drunken act of rage that made him pick up the gun and fire it through the windowpanes in the direction of the stable where his father had gone. Let the reader decide.

His unfortunate mother was in the line of fire, the rest is history.

RICHARD THOMAS PARKER POSTSCRIPT

One of the first clues highlighting Parker's degenerate behaviour can be found in the Nottinghamshire Guardian dated Thursday the 13th of November 1856, eight years before the shooting, where amongst the District News, the Southwell Petty Sessions reported:

Thomas Parker of Fiskerton was charged with being drunk at Rolleston during divine service, on 19th ult (last month). *Fined 5s and costs. (equivalent in 2020 = £23.53).* It can only be left to the imagination as to what occurred on that particular Sunday.

Over the next few years, his antics must have continued in much the same manner, as he admitted himself that he was no stranger to the lock-up.

And so, from the drunken episode in church onwards, we can begin to piece together Parker's demise. At the time of the 1861 census, he lived on Stodman Street, Newark, with his wife Emily, his occupation was recorded as 'Butcher.'

Their daughter Julia was baptised on the 14th of July 1861 at St Mary's, Newark, their abode is recorded as Stodman Street. Sixteen months later, their son Samuel was baptised on the 9th of November 1862 at St Mary's, Newark. Their abode at this point is recorded as Fiskerton, suggesting Parker now occupied the butcher's shop his father gave him in the Spread Eagle yard opposite his parents' house. However, as local and national newspapers reported, the business could not have lasted long, and proof of this can be found in the London Gazette, dated the 2nd of December 1862. It read as follows:

[8]*Richard Thomas Parker of Fiskerton, in the county of Nottingham, Butcher, having been adjudged bankrupt under petition for adjudication of Bankruptcy, filed in the County Court of Nottinghamshire, holden at Newark, on the 10th day of November,*

1862, a public sitting, for the said bankrupt to pass his last Examination and make application for his Discharge, will be held before Richard Wildman, Esq., the Judge of the said Court, on the 20th day of December instant, at the County Sessions-room, Newark, at ten of the clock in the forenoon precisely, the day last aforesaid being the day limited for the said bankrupt to surrender, William Newton is the Official Assignee and William Edward Ashley, of Newark, is the Solicitor acting in the bankruptcy.

Mr Newton, if you remember, was also the coroner at Mrs Parker's inquest, and Mr Ashley stood for the defence at Richard Thomas Parker's trial. It would appear that they both knew Parker well.

And so, it would seem that the slippery path of Parker's decline had already commenced, and within the space of four years, he went from married man with a family and a business, to a convicted criminal, hanged for the murder of his mother.

Six weeks after Parker's execution, the London Gazette announced:

Richard Thomas Parker, of Fiskerton, in the county of Nottingham, Butcher, adjudicated bankrupt on the 10th day of November, 1862. A Dividend Meeting will be held on the 5th day of October next, at twelve o'clock noon precisely.

THE AFTERMATH

So, what happened to the rest of the Parker family and associates following the tragic events of 1864?

EMILY PARKER - formerly PETTIFAR

Although great affection had been demonstrated between Richard Thomas Parker and his wife Emily at the end, she was now free from her brutal husband with the prospect of re-building a new life for herself and her children. Hope for this came about eighteen months after the execution when she married George Flower on the 27th of February 1866 at St Mary's, Newark. The parish register records Emily as a widow, and it would be so pleasing to think that she might have found happiness with George Flower, whose occupation was poetically, 'Nursery and Seedsman,' however, it was not meant to be.

Emily died at only thirty-three years of age and had been married to George Flower for a mere four years. The certificate records her death date and place as, '*1 June 1870, Market Place,* the cause of death '*Gastritis - 3 months.*' She was buried on the 3rd of June 1870 at St Mary's, Newark... Poor Emily.

THE CHILDREN – SAMUEL AND JULIA

The 1871 census tells us that Emily's son, Samuel, now eight years old, was still being cared for by George Flower, who had re-married very soon after Emily died... to another Emily. Meanwhile, Julia, now nine years of age, was staying with her grandparents, the Pettifars, at 22 Victoria Street, Newark.

According to the 1881 census, both children, now in their late teens, were living at 18 Wilson Street, Newark, and Samuel continued in the gardening trade. Julia was recorded as an annuitant, someone who receives an annual sum of money, possibly from her late grandfather's estate.

But the tragedy continued...

Samuel died aged only nineteen of '*Pulmonary Phthisis - 1 year,*' he was buried on the 4th of May 1882 at St Mary's, Newark. His death certificate records him as the '*son of Thomas Parker - a Butcher (deceased').* How much sadness the Parker family must have suffered during this time is very hard to comprehend.

It would seem Julia fared much better, she married a schoolteacher named George Kirkby on the 26th of March 1883 in Newark. Her father was also recorded as Thomas Parker, deceased, on the certificate. Soon after their marriage, Julia and George moved to Whitstable in Kent and had three children, Robert George, born in 1884, William Arthur in 1885 and Mabel Emily in 1888.

Perhaps a fresh start in a new place had been required for Julia as the family appeared to flourish, and by the 1911 census, George had reached the status of Head Teacher.

SAMUEL PARKER - Senior

How Samuel coped in the years after his son's execution is unknown, but one could easily imagine him a broken man. There were fears that he became very ill after the execution, but a statement made in the Nottinghamshire Guardian on Friday the 19th of August 1864 read as follows:

THE FISKERTON TRAGEDY

There is no foundation for the statement that Mr Parker of Fiskerton has been suffering from a serious illness since the execution of his unhappy son. The old man has been in his usual health but is of course deeply afflicted at the sad tragedy which has deprived him of both wife and son. He, however, attends to his business as usual and some of his relatives constantly reside with him.

Samuel was still recorded as a farmer in Fiskerton in the 1864 White's Directory, however, Morris and Co.'s 1869 Directory of Grantham, Chesterfield and Gainsborough informs us that Samuel Parker, now in his late sixties, was no longer listed at Fiskerton.

From the document *ref: DD 899/3,* deposited at the Nottinghamshire Archives, which gives details of the sales and purchases of the land and properties of the Spread Eagle Yard, it can be learned that Samuel sold his house in 1865 to Mrs Haynes, his friend and neighbour.

The 1871 and 1881 census returns show Samuel living in Sneinton with his brother Matthew, recorded as a 'Retired Farmer' and 'Wheelwright', respectively. At the time of Samuel's death on the 8th of October 1884, he was living with his nephew Matthew, the son of his brother Matthew, at 2 Ireton Square, off Portland Road, Nottingham.

In his last will and testament, Samuel devises all his real estate *'whatsoever and wheresoever to the uses following (that is to say) to the use that my sister Charlotte Foster* (one of the aunts who visited Parker in prison) *may receive thereout during her life a yearly rent Charge of eight pounds'* (equivalent in 2020 = £840.10). The remainder of his personal estate amounting to £41 5s 0d *(equivalent in 2020 = £4332)* was left to the *'said nephew Matthew.'* Not a vast sum after everything Samuel had endured.

One explanation could be supported by an article in the Nottinghamshire Guardian a couple of months after the execution. It read, *'Some complaints were made of the insufficient expenses allowed by the Clerk of Assize in reference to the prosecution of the late Richard Thomas Parker.'* The report talks about the expense of hiring *'flies'* (hansom cabs) to visit Fiskerton on several occasions and *'it was rather unreasonable that the expense of these flies should be paid for by the Clerk of the Magistrates out of his own pocket.'*

Incredibly the next statement relates to the medical bills. *'A gentleman was required to attend from Newark and examine the progress the sufferers were making before the prisoner's commitment, and it was not fair that this expense should fall on the Clerk of the Magistrates. No doubt a considerable portion of the medical bill would have to be paid by the man who recovered, Parker himself.'* There was a comment that *'the doctor was not sent for by Parker,'* but how the matter was resolved was not reported, and one can only guess whether poor Samuel ended up paying out of his own pocket or not.

During the last twenty years of his life, Samuel witnessed the murder of his wife at the hands of their own son, the execution of his doomed son, suffered the loss of his daughter-in-law, and then his only grandson.

Samuel is buried in the General Cemetery, Nottingham, his nephew Matthew is also in the same grave. Mrs Elizabeth Parker is buried at the Holy Trinity Church, Rolleston.

MARY HAYNES

Mrs Haynes had been the Parker's neighbour since at least the 1851 census. She and her husband, James, who was also the ferryman, ran the grocer's shop in Fiskerton. James died in 1863 and left Mary *'effects under £100'* (*equivalent in 2020 = £9639*). Mary kept the shop until sometime between the 1871 and 1881 censuses, and after her death on the 11th of July 1885 at Melton Street, Nottingham, she bequeathed a mere £2 (*equivalent in 2020 = £217.60*) to her grandson, James.

HANNAH BURDEN

Hannah came from Plungar in Leicestershire and was a dressmaker before becoming the Parker's servant, having only been in their employ for about a year when the tragic events of 1864 took place. Very soon after, Hannah must have gone back home to Plungar, where she married Edward Porter on the 14th of June 1864. The tragedy must have left its mark, so much so that she named her two sons Samuel and Tom.

Perhaps it is a coincidence, but...

P.C. GEORGE BARKSBY

Before his elevation to the ranks of Police Constable, George began his working life as a farm servant in Trowell. He then became the local policeman in various villages, including Cropwell Bishop, Farndon, and then on to Fiskerton. Following his encounter with the Parker family, he was next found in East Leake, ending his days in East Retford.

He died on the 14th of May 1891, aged fifty-eight and left a personal estate of £205 0s 4d (*equivalent in 2020 = £22,560*) to his widow, Hannah.

CORNELIUS DONCASTER

An upstanding citizen was Cornelius, not only was he the landlord of the Spread Eagle Inn, but he was also the enumerator on the 1861 census of Fiskerton. Nevertheless, a minor indiscretion occurred during his career in March 1855, when he was charged with *'keeping open his house past 12 o'clock.'* Fortunately, *'several witnesses were called by the defendant to prove that he ceased filling or drawing drink before 12 o'clock'* and the charges were dropped, but he was strongly admonished by the bench. Cornelius died on the 8th of May 1865, aged forty-five, less than a year after the tragic events that occurred in the Spread Eagle Yard. He left effects of *'under £200.'* (*equivalent in 2020 = £19,260*)

SIR COLIN JUSTICE BLACKBURN – JUDGE AT THE TRIAL

Sir Colin was born in Bonhill, Dunbarton, Scotland, on the 18th of May 1813, the second son of John and Rebecca. He received a privileged education at Edinburgh Academy and Eton and Trinity College, Cambridge, graduating as 8th [9]Wrangler in 1835.

He was called to the bar in 1838, and after a slow start in his legal career, he was unexpectedly given the position of puisne judge at the Court of Queen's Bench in 1859. He soon proved himself to be a very sound lawyer, and after being knighted in 1860, he went on to become the first appointed Lord of Appeal in 1876. That same year he was created Baron Blackburn of Killearn, Stirlingshire.

Said about Colin Blackburn from Wikipedia: *'Though greatly respected he does not seem to have been popular; according to a well-known story he informed a colleague that he intended to retire in vacation to avoid the trouble of a retirement dinner - the colleague cheerfully replied that this was quite unnecessary since no-one would have turned up to the dinner anyway.'*

Sir Colin remained unmarried throughout his life and died on the 8th of January 1896, aged eighty-two, thus his life peerage became extinct.

WILLIAM EDWARD ASHLEY - SOLICITOR

Mr Ashley can be found living in Newark from the 1851 census onwards, but no wife or children are recorded in any census returns. Despite his somewhat unsuccessful defence plea for reducing Parker's sentence to manslaughter, it would appear that Mr Ashley was extremely successful with other clients. This is reflected in the rather large sum of his personal estate following his death on the 18th of October 1883. It totalled £17,715 6s 3d. *(equivalent in 2019 = £1,797,000)* With no wife or family, I wonder who the lucky recipients were.

WILLIAM NEWTON - SOLICITOR AND CORONER

Mr Newton also resided in Newark, and the 1864 White's Directory tells us that alongside his other duties as solicitor and coroner, he was also Clerk to the Magistrates. However, like Mr Ashley, no children are mentioned on any census returns, and Mr Newton was widowed by the 1891 census. He died on the 6th of February 1899, and the probate record states, *Probate Nottingham 19th May to Samuel Jones solicitor, Effects £26,959 2s 1d. (equivalent in 2020 = £3,057,000)*

SERGEANT O'BRIEN

The term Sergeant in this context refers to Mr O'Brien being a Sergeant-at-Law. Held in high legal esteem since the days of Henry II (1154-1189) when he created the order. They rose in power, becoming an elite body of lawyers who carried out most of the work in the common courts of law. However, during the reign of Elizabeth I (1558-1603), the Queen's Counsel was created, after which the number of Sergeants-at-Law began to decline. The Judicature Act of 1873, which came into force in 1875, brought about the re-organization of the English Justice system, abolishing the appointment of Sergeants.

The Sergeant-at-Law hired to defend Richard Thomas Parker was Michael O'Brien, a well-known lawyer on the Midland Circuit. The same Sergeant O'Brien had defended Townley the year before for a fee of 75 guineas (*equivalent in 2020 = £7800*), so we could assume the Parker family forfeited a similar fee.

Michael O'Brien was born in about 1813 in Tipperary, Ireland and can be found in the 1861 census of England living in Paddington, London, with his wife, Bessie. His occupation is listed as 'Barrister-at-law practising.' He had been a member of Lincoln's Inn until the 20th of May 1862, after which he joined the Sergeants Inn.

Mr O'Brien died in 1873 in Brighton, Sussex and surprisingly, bearing in mind the fees he would have been earning and his status as a lawyer, his effects were under £200 *(equivalent in 2020= £17,850)* Not quite the sum you would expect when compared to that of Messrs Newton and Ashley.

ROBERT SWINSCOE

Born in about 1839, Robert Swinscoe lived in Morton, the neighbouring village to Fiskerton. He was the friend whom Richard Thomas Parker suggested should change his ways, and from reading various newspaper reports, it would appear Swinscoe had every reason to do as his friend requested.

The first encounter with Swinscoe appeared in the Nottinghamshire Guardian on the 6th of September 1860, when it was reported that *'a man drowned at Fiskerton Ferry.'* The unfortunate man was George Clark, aged twenty-nine, a drinking colleague of Swinscoe. On Sunday the 19th of August 1860, the pair had crossed the river in the ferry boat to visit Taylor's at Stoke for a glass of gin and a cigar, after which *'they got into the company'* of two girls. The young men had then gone their separate ways. It was later that evening when George, who had already crossed the river earlier, refused to fetch the ferryman to bring Swinscoe back over, saying he would do it himself when he apparently fell out of the boat and drowned. It was reported that George was *'in liquor'* at the time. His body was discovered the next day in a willow holt near Muskham.

The Southwell Petty Sessions go on to reveal a list of charges against Swinscoe:

25th July 1862 - charged alongside five others with assaulting Michael Fox at Morton. Each man was made to pay 7s costs *(equivalent in 2020 = £32.90)* and cautioned.

6th of March 1863 - ordered to pay the costs after assaulting Jane Johnson at Morton.

26th June 1863 - Swinscoe and three more 'mates' were charged with breach of the peace at Fiskerton. This involved some fighting in the fields following a drinking session at The Spread Eagle Inn, the result of which led to Cornelius Doncaster also being charged with allowing *'drunkenness and other disorderly conduct in his house.'*

The next mention of Swinscoe in March 1868 shows a turn in events at the Petty Sessions when it is he who accuses William Elliot of using threatening language against him. The same report adds that there had been several *'maiden sessions of late'* where no criminal charges had been brought forth, which spoke well for the area.

In the 1871 census, Swinscoe can be found living in Lincolnshire working as an Engine

Driver and is now a married man. However, he still gets a mention in the Lincolnshire Chronicle on the 7th of October 1870 when he charges Joseph Bailey with '*breach of contract at Billinghay.*'

By the 1881 census, he lived in Yorkshire and had fathered four children, however, he still could not keep his name out of the newspaper. To be fair, this time, he was called as a witness to a drunken episode in 1879 at the New Inn, Wadsley-Bridge, Sheffield. A group of men were summoned for being found drunk on licensed premises, and Swinscoe, an '*engine-tenter,*' stated that he was at the New Inn on the Saturday afternoon '*for about three hours and during that time all the defendants were supplied with drink until they became very drunk and quarrelsome.*'

By the 1891 census, he had returned to Fiskerton with his children, he was now widowed, and his occupation recorded as '*late threshing machine engine driver.*' He died two years later, in 1893, aged fifty-six.

Whether he altered his path in life and gave his heart to God, as his friend Parker had implored, one can only guess.

CHARLES RICHARDSON

Although not an integral part of the story, spare a thought for poor Charles if you can. He was one of the signed and sworn executors of John Parker's estate in 1871, John being one of the "notoriously insane uncles" mentioned earlier (page 16). Charles was married to John's sister Mary.

Reading from a newspaper clipping in the Nottinghamshire Guardian from Friday the 17th of March 1876, it transpires that Mr Richardson of Thurgarton '*neglected to carry out the text and particulars of the will by having the money in the Southwell bank. He did it at the request of the widow and received 4 per cent for it. He had had threatening letters from the solicitors and got it into his head that they would take proceedings against him and nothing could stop them; that he should have the money to pay and should come to distress.*'

For several months, Mr Richardson had become very low-spirited and despondent about the bank, and at four o'clock on Tuesday, the previous week had said he was going to church to fetch some books. Apparently, he sometimes stayed out late and had '*always taken a little drink.*' Tragically, he was discovered by his son and his brother the following morning at about seven o'clock, hanging in the tower of Thurgarton church by the bell rope. They cut him down, but *'he was dead - stiff and cold. Nothing was disarranged; he appeared to have jumped off the seat, and he just touched the ground with his toes.'* The inquest returned a verdict of *'suicide whilst in a state of temporary insanity.'*

So, if insanity supposedly ran in the Parker family, it also seems to have rubbed off on those who married into the family... Poor Charles.

THOMAS ASKERNE - EXECUTIONER

Last but not least, born in 1816, most facts to be found about Thomas Askerne seem to focus mainly on his later career as an Executioner and how he had taken up the position whilst in York Debtors Prison. This was the usual way of recruiting executioners, the inmate would volunteer for the role as a way of escaping their prison sentence. Surprisingly, Askerne's previous occupation was a policeman,

It seems that Mr Askerne was not particularly good at his new choice of career. It was reported that Richard Thomas Parker 'died hard' and many others fell foul of Askerne's bungled attempts too. He mainly officiated at York's executions, but he also worked further afield, including five public hangings in Durham. The last of these was Matthew Atkinson on the 16th of March 1865. The rope broke as he dropped, and he had to be hanged for a second time. Askerne was not selected again at Durham after this incident.

Only a couple of months before Parker's fateful day, George Bryce suffered at the hands of Askerne in Scotland, when he measured a drop too short and Bryce was left struggling, slowly strangling to death, and was not declared dead until forty minutes later. The crowd became so incensed that a riot nearly broke out, and Askerne had to be disguised and smuggled out of the city.

His list of botched hangings continued until that of John Henry Johnson on the 3rd of April 1877 at Armley. Again, the rope broke and once again, the second attempt left Johnson strangling to death. Askerne was sacked after this last debacle.

He died on the 6th of December 1878 in Maltby, Yorkshire, aged sixty-two.

The last hangings in Britain took place on the 13th of August 1964, and the death sentence was finally abolished in 1965.

PREVIOUS EXECUTIONS IN NOTTINGHAM

As listed in the Nottinghamshire Guardian Supplement on the 12th of August 1864

1101 - John de Cuckney

1212 - The Welsh hostages, twenty-eight noble youths hanged by order of King John from the ramparts of the Castle

1685 - Joan Philips for highway robbery

1701 - Timothy Buckley for highway robbery and killing a gentleman and his footman

1720 - Richard Comyn for uttering a base coin

1727 - Robert Pemberton for burglary in the premises now on Long Row

1728 - John Briggs for killing his wife

1729 - John Revell Esq for shooting a trespasser at Papplewick

1732 - William Pycroft for coining

1735 - Henry Parnell for wife murder at Cotgrave

1737 - James Gibbins for highway robbery

1738 - Thomas Hallam for cow stealing at Wilford

1748 - Smith and Miller for highway robbery

1752 - James Wogden 'Innocent Jemmy' for the murder of Edward Whatman near Ollerton

1753 - Woolston Roberts and William Sandham soldiers for maiming a recruit

1757 - Richard Sturgess for robbing his employers

1758 - Robert Wilson for robbing Sarah Maud a pedlar

1759 - William Andrew Horne Esq for the murder of his incestuous child

1759 - Samuel Ward for breaking into a house on Byard Lane

1763 - Elizabeth Morton fifteen years of age for strangling a child

1766 - James Bromage and William Wainer for highway robbery

1767 - Robert Downe for killing a boy at Mansfield

1767 - Thomas Reynolds for burglary in Chesterfield Street

1770 - William Hebb for the murder of Mr Burrill of Newark

1773 - Joseph Shaw for burglary in Long Row

1774 - Richard Wheatley for robbery and return from transportation

1775 - William Voce for violating and killing Mary Dufty

1779 - John Spencer for killing William and Mary Yeadon at Scrooby

1781 - George Brown and Adam Bagshaw for burglary at Kirkby Woodhouse

1782 - Cooper Hall for robbing the Tuxford to Newark mail cart

1784 - Ann Castledine and Robert Rushton the former for infanticide and the latter for the murder of his daughter

1784 - Thomas Henfrey and William Rider for highway robbery at Plungar

1785 - John Pendril, John Townsend, John Anderson and William Cook—the last-named for horse stealing, the three others for highway robbery

1785 - Thomas Cobb for burglary in Normanton-on-Trent

1786 - William Hands and John Lister the former for horse stealing, the latter for sheep stealing

1790 - Samuel Martin and Anthony Farnsworth for robbing the warehouse of Messrs, John Heard & Co

1793 - William Healy for horse stealing

1795 - David Proctor for violating the person of his step-daughter aged ten years

1797 - John Milner for cow stealing at Rufford

1799 - James Brodie, a blind man for killing his guide boy near Mansfield

1800 - John Atkinson for forgery

1801 - Michael Denman, William Sykes and Thomas Bakewell—the two first for burglary at Mansfield and the last for burglary at Sutton Bonnington

1802 - Ferdinando Davis for highway robbery at Lenton

1803 - John Thompson for stealing a portmanteau at Newark

1803 - William Hill for violating the person of Mrs Sarah Justice

1805 - Robert Powell *alias* Harvey for burglary at Worksop

1806 - William Rhodes *alias* Davies for forgery

1809 - Thomas Lampin for forging a bill of exchange at Newark

1812 - Benjamin Renshaw for stack burning at Mansfield

1813 - William Simpson for housebreaking at Watnall

1815 - John Hemstock *alias* Black for the murder of James Snell near Retford

1816 - John Simpson for highway robbery at Mansfield and Eastwood

1817 - Daniel Diggle for shooting at Mr George Kerrey

1817 - Charles Rotherham for the murder of Elizabeth Shepherd near Newstead

1818 - George Needham and William Mandeville for house robbery at Burton Joyce and Thurgarton

1820 - Thomas Wilcox for highway robbery at Chilwell

1822 - Henry Sanderson, Robert Bamford and Adam Adie, the first for the murder of William Carr at Walting-Wells and the two last for the murder of John Timms by throwing him off the Trent Bridge

1823 - Thomas Roe and Benjamin Miller for highway robbery near Arnold

1825 - Thomas Dewey for the murder of Mrs Austin in Brook Street

1826 - Samuel Wood for the murder of his wife on Parliament Row

1826 - George Milnes and Joshua Smith *alias* Shepherd for burglary near Retford

1827 - William Wells for highway robbery

1831 - William Reynolds and William Marshall for violating the person of Mary Ann Lord

1832 - George Beck, George Hearson and John Armstrong for firing the silk mill at Beeston

1833 - William Clayton - for the wilful murder of Samuel Kay at Sutton-cum-Lound

1834 - William Hinckley for the murder of his wife in Bold Lane

1835 - Richard Smith *alias* Jones for violating the person of Mary Green aged fourteen

1839 - John Driver for the murder of Mrs Hancock at Caunton

1842 - John Jones *alias* Moore for the murder of Mary Hallam at Mansfield

1844 - William Saville for the murder of his wife and three children at Colwick

1860 - John Fenton for the murder of Charles Spencer at Walkeringham

Acknowledgements

Even though the internet has opened up a whole new world of family history research, there is still such a wealth of information waiting to be discovered at our local Archives and Libraries. I always feel so excited when uncovering an old document or record bearing one of my ancestor's names. With that in mind, I can never thank the staff at the Nottinghamshire Archives enough whenever I venture there. I like to consider them as the "font of all knowledge" as they always have an answer to any question I ask of them.

Likewise, I would like to thank members of staff at the University of Nottingham, Manuscripts and Special Collections Department, who are equally as patient and helpful.

Many thanks to Paul Mann QC for his input regarding legal terms, Sergeants-at-law, the 19th-century justice system, and two thoroughly enjoyable evenings attending his presentations on the subject of the Fiskerton Murder. Also, to His Honour, Judge Milmo QC, for steering me in the direction of the correct Sergeant O'Brien.

Also, a big thank you to Steve Wells for the illustrations of Mrs Parker's skull.

References

[1] PE46/20 Sculcoates All Saints marriage register 1810-1812 held by (East Ridings Archives and Local Studies)

[2] Nottinghamshire Archives Ref: DDM 105/107 Depositions

[3] Nottinghamshire Archives Ref: DDM 105/107 Depositions

[4] Nottinghamshire Archives Ref: DDM 105/113 Post-Mortem

[5] Nottinghamshire Archives Ref: DDM 105/107 Depositions

[6] Nottinghamshire Archives DDM 105/118 Charge

[7] William Saville brutally murdered his wife and children with a cut-throat razor on the 21st of May 1844 in Colwick Woods, Nottingham

[8] from: www.london-gazette.co.uk

[9] a Wrangler is a student who gained a first-class honours degree in Mathematics at Cambridge University.

All money equivalents are calculated using the Purchasing Power calculator on *www.measuringworth.com*

About the Author

I began researching my family history in 2006 and was extremely fortunate that my Mum and Dad were still around to tell me their memories, of which there were many. Like most family trees, there are illegitimate children, numerous hasty marriages, and even money in one branch of my tree during the Georgian period, all spent and forgotten now.

Some mysteries have yet to be solved, and others have been substantiated with evidence, and when my Mum remembered her father telling her about the ancestor who was hanged for murder, that definitely required further investigation.

Not knowing our distant ancestors, yet having snippets of information about their lives, I love using my imagination to write what might have happened. I am looking forward to sharing those stories with you over time.

Other books by Emmaline Severn available on Amazon

GLORIA

A novel telling how Gloria's emotionally charged life shapes her transition from girl to woman as she steers her family through both world wars and into post-war Britain. An epic tale of love, loss, betrayal, family and friendship.

5-star reviews –

- A touching, roller-coaster life story of a headstrong woman
- Poignant life story
- A thoroughly enjoyable and compelling read

"STEADY AS SHE GOES"

The poignant wartime memories of a WWII navy 'medic'

Told as a touching conversation between father and daughter in his latter years, this short story recounts his memories of that time.

Also written by the author with The Field Detectives under the name of Catherine Pincott-Allen.

A FURTHER ACCOUNT OF THE HACKER FAMILY

In sixteenth and seventeenth-century England, the Hacker family were powerful and wealthy people - owning substantial amounts of property and land and exerting significant influence throughout Nottinghamshire and the Midlands in such places as East Bridgford, Colston Bassett and Stathern. That all changed in 1660 when Colonel Francis Hacker was executed for the part he played in the regicide of King Charles I almost eleven years earlier.

The book traces the origins of the family from Yeovil, Somerset and follows its progress to the grisly death of Francis, and beyond.

In this revised edition, the author has made a number of new revelations about the family which challenge conventional thinking that has built up for more than 300 years. At the heart of this focused historical research, is the story of a family that was broken apart by the ravages of the English Civil Wars and pulled together by strong personalities whose values and commitment to one another overcame the prejudices of the age in which they lived.

It makes for compelling reading.

5-star reviews
- Excellent research. First class read
- A new viewpoint on history